The Spiritual Tool Chest

Volume 1: Meditations

The Spiritual Tool Chest

Volume 1: Meditations

Nathaniel Altman

Gaupo Publishing
Brooklyn, New York
www.gaupo.net

GAUPO PUBLISHING

The Spiritual Tool Chest: Volume 1: Meditations

Nathaniel Altman

This volume is the first part of a revised edition of *The Little Giant Encyclopedia of Meditations and Blessings*, originally published by Sterling Publishing Co. Inc. in 2000.

Published in the United States by Gaupo Publishing.

ISBN 978-0-9979720-1-6

Dedicated to the memory of

José Alberto Rosa, M.D.

Table of Contents

Preface viii

Introduction 1
Foundations 9
   Creating Sacred Space 9
   Meditation Postures 15
   Basic Relaxation Exercises 21
   Breathing 24
   Keeping a Journal 28
Alignment Meditation 30
Rachel's Meditation Technique 32
Basic Zazen Meditation 32
Thought Meditation 37
Empty Space Meditation 38
Meditating for Mind Expansion 38
Candle Meditation 40
Meditation on Sacred Symbols 41
Word Symbol Meditation 44
Meditating to Music 46
Energy Meditations 47
The Four Facets of Loving 49
The Eightfold Path Meditation 52
Mantra Meditations 55
A Simple Christian Meditation 69
The Centering Prayer Meditation 71
Listening to the Divine 72
Forgiveness Meditations 73
Goodness Meditation 77
Meditations of Gratitude 78
Angel Meditations 79
Guardian Angel Meditations 82
Eating Meditation 85

Meditation for Drivers 87
Airplane Meditations 89
Meditations for Right Livelihood 91
Healing Meditations 93
Outdoor Meditation to
    Aid in Transforming Feelings 111
Tree of Life - Kabbalah Meditation 112
Nature Meditations 115
Meditations on the Four Elements 118
Flower Meditations 121
Tree Meditations 125
Water Meditations 132
Meditating on Numbers 135
Walking Meditations 138
T'ai Chi Chuan Meditations 145
Seeking Wisdom 147
Daily Review Meditations 149
The Golden Stairs 153
Meditations on the Seven Rays 154
Hawk Meditation 158
Visiting the Mansion 159
"Getting to Know Your Potential Self"
    Meditation 160
Chakra Meditations 163
Rainbow Color Meditations 174
Meditations for Deepening Love and
    Enhancing Sexual Expression 177
A Group Meditation 186
Acknowledgements 189
About the Author /Compiler 190

Preface

When asked a question about personal transformation, Hugh Lynn Cayce, eldest son of the famous seer Edgar Cayce, answered, "If I had to give a person one suggestion as to how to alter or raise his consciousness, it would be to practice prayer and meditation. I don't know of anything that would mean more."

Meditation, prayer and blessing are powerful tools that provide a multitude of benefits. Recent studies have shown that regular meditation can reduce stress, lower blood pressure, reduce physical pain, and improve memory and mental focus. In addition to providing solace in times of need, prayer has been used throughout human history to help people tread the often difficult path of healing and integration. Evidence gleaned from literally hundreds of controlled medical trials has shown that prayer can greatly enhance the body's innate ability to heal itself of a wide range of health problems, including heart disease and cancer.

Mindy Ribner, the founder of the Jewish Meditation Circle in New York City, once observed, "Prayer and meditation go together like the inhalation and exhalation of the breath. A good meditation is often sandwiched between words of prayer, just as heartfelt prayer is preceded and followed by meditation."

By practicing prayer and meditation- even if only a few minutes a day- we can enhance our lives in a powerful and lasting way. Achieving a greater sense of inner peace, increased mental awareness, reduced stress, and stronger feelings of optimism and purpose are only some of the reported benefits of daily spiritual practices such as prayer, meditation and sending blessings to others. These practices not only help us enjoy a more fulfilling life, but can have a great impact on the lives of those around us.

The book you have before you is the first of a two-volume "tool chest" to help you develop your own spiritual practice. It is devoted to the art and science of meditation, which can be defined as a way of focusing our consciousness to see the world more clearly. It is also a way of linking ourselves to others. In contrast to prayer, which usually involves an outward appeal to what is variously known as God, the Higher Source, or the Great Spirit, meditation is intended to open yourself to this Higher Source, as well as to your own spiritual power within.

This volume will include many different types of meditation techniques drawn from a wide variety of spiritual traditions, including guided meditations, meditating on sacred symbols, meditating to music, chanting, Zazen meditation, walking meditations, candle meditations, meditations in nature, writing meditations, Tantric meditations and healing meditations.

The Spiritual Tool Chest is intended to show, in part, that treasures are to be found throughout the spectrum of religious diversity. While you, the reader, may be primarily drawn to meditations that reflect your own spiritual tradition, you might also consider the offerings of other spiritual traditions as well, if only to gain a deeper understanding and appreciation of the beliefs of other members of the human family. It is hoped that this book will become your spiritual companion that you can consult at any time for any need.

Meditation- along with prayer and blessing- enables us to communicate with what Abraham Lincoln called during his First Inaugural Address "the better angels of our nature," thus allowing us to make wiser and more compassionate choices in our lives. As we are all cells in the body of humanity, the positive changes that meditation can bring us as individuals can affect everyone we have contact with every single day.

Malcolm Gladwell described the "tipping point" as the moment when a social trend crosses a threshold and starts to spread like wildfire. At this critical time in human history, the goals of peace, understanding and harmony may appear unattainable to many. Yet if enough individuals joyfully engage in the regular practice of meditation- along with prayer and blessing- a tipping point can occur when their positive effects can spread throughout the world and transform human society.

Nathaniel Altman
Brooklyn, New York
May 2017

Introduction

Today's world seems to be moving faster and faster. Despite labor-saving devices like computers and smart phones, we seem to work longer hours than ever before. Many of us find it difficult to balance work, quality time with our family and precious time by ourselves. We are becoming increasingly bombarded by information, opinions and hype from the media, advertising and the Internet. And in an age of material abundance, many of us are unhappy. We want "something more" in our lives.

Meditation is a way of helping us to see the outer world -and ourselves- more clearly. It is also a way to help us learn to relate to our family, friends and co-workers in a deeper and more meaningful way.

Meditation has been called "mindful awareness:" a consciousness of both the world around is as well as our own inner world, with its drama, conflicts and fears. It is also an awareness of the calmer, intelligent "inner essence" that some religions call the soul.

Over the past few years, an increasing amount of research has been done revealing the many benefits of meditation. On a purely physical level, regular meditation practice has been found to help:

-lower blood pressure
-reduce anxiety and stress
-improve immune system function
-increase energy and stamina
-help manage asthma flare ups and other allergic
    reactions
-manage pain

1

Many meditators have reported lasting mental and psychological benefits as well. They include:

- increased ability to be calm
- improved mental focus
- expanded mental perspectives
- greater empathy and compassion for others
- enhanced creativity
- improved memory
- improved sleep
- deeper contact with one's spiritual essence
- reduced use/interest in drugs and alcohol
- greater feelings of optimism
- greater efficiency at work and school
- a clearer sense of one's personal goals

Lower Self, Higher Self

A noted psychologist once wrote that the human mind is a complex and amazing thing. There is some truth to his opinion. We humans have the ability to live in different states of reality, which can vary from each other tremendously. On one hand, we have an often childlike side that always thinks of itself. This side is often vain, selfish, opinionated and destructive. Its time frame is confined to the here and now, not unlike a spoiled (but perhaps likeable) child whose needs demand their parent's immediate attention.

While this part of ourselves often gets us into trouble, it also tends to make our life more interesting. Spiritual teachers have called this part of us the "lower self," which looks out for its interests and wants to have its own way at any cost.

We also have another side to our nature that is

known variously as the universal self, the higher self, or the "spark of God within." More quiet and subtle than the lower self, it possesses superior wisdom, love and strength that are inclusive, compassionate and ageless. Sometimes we are lucky enough to know an older, wise person who has lived their life and is a source of common sense, practical wisdom and infinite patience. This person accepts us the way we are without judgment, and is happy to offer counsel, which is always wise and helpful. Such an elder is a source of calm and stability in an often crazy world.

The higher self is not unlike that special person. No matter what time of the day or night- or wherever we happen to be- we can go there for comfort, wisdom and inspiration.

In addition to the higher self and the lower self, we also possess the will and knowledge of the mind. When it comes to meditation, this part of our makeup is very important, because it can help us achieve several important goals:

1. It allows us to observe the childlike destructive side of ourselves and see how it lives its daily life through attitudes, ideas, fears, emotions and activities that cause us conflicts, keep us separate from others, undermines our happiness, and prevents us from being integrated and whole human beings.

2. At the same time, it can open us to the universal, unlimited part of our being. This not only allows us to contact deeper realities, but enables us to confront and eventually transform negative currents that make us anxious, fearful, angry and generally unhappy.

3

3. Rather than make us holy, meditation helps us realize that we are *already holy*: it enables us to see more clearly who we already are.

Meditation: The Key

A spiritual teacher wrote that we create our own reality by the sum total of our feelings, our conscious (and subconscious) opinions and our personal attitudes and goals. Taken together, these thoughts, attitudes and emotions determine our actions in daily life, as well as our reactions to what is going on around us. According to a booklet published by Meditation Group for the New Age (now Meditation Mount) in Ojai, California:

> Every human action is the result of some inner activity. All too often it is our desires and uncontrolled thoughts which drive us, and this can bring about all sorts of difficulties and even have harmful consequences, both for the individual and for mankind in general. This is why it is essential to become the masters of our own inner realm, creating in this subjective world only what we consider to be right and constructive and contributing to the common good on these inner planes as much as we would in the outer world. Many of us experience our inner life as a tangled mass of contradictory thoughts and feelings. We often indulge in fear and negative thinking, which causes us anxiety and pain. Most of us are the source of literally hundreds of negative thoughts, angry emotions, and hurtful

attitudes every single day. Even if we could make the charitable claim that if half the people over the age of 12 alive today are responsible for at least ten negative thoughts, attitudes or actions every day, it should not be surprising that our world has often become a violent, insecure and unhealthy place to live.

By the same token, by dedicating ourselves to challenging wrong ideas, letting go of unhelpful emotional patterns and dealing with destructive feelings in a spirit of honesty and courage, we not only create a new life for ourselves, but we benefit every living being on earth. Meditation is the key that begins this magical process.

A Creative Endeavor

This is why meditation is considered an essentially creative endeavor. Since our attitudes, feelings and beliefs are constantly manifesting themselves in our world every single day, our most important task is to *become aware* of what we think, how we feel and what we believe.

Though not always comfortable, we especially need to become aware of those negative thoughts and feelings that are hidden from view, because their power is greatest when we don't know (or merely suspect) that they are there.

At the same time, we need to acknowledge and honor our positive thoughts and feelings, and allow them fuller expression. Like a gardener who nurtures a tiny acorn until it is able to grow into a powerful oak tree, we need to nurture our positive thoughts and feelings until they become a dominant aspect of our nature.

Whenever we focus on what is going on inside and observe our inner landscapes in greater detail our awareness of *who we really are* is strengthened. We also contact what teachers call "the infinite self," which helps us to become more integrated and whole. It allows us to transform negative attitudes, destructive emotions and wrong beliefs into positive qualities that bring more excitement, integration and happiness into our lives. According to the spiritual teacher H. Saraydarian:

> Thus meditation must be handled as a part of our daily life. In all our activity, expression and relationships, meditation has to be present, not as an object by itself, but as a vital factor in all undertakings. As with any other skill, meditation works best when practiced daily. In time, we become more able to tap into the wellspring of unlimited love and wisdom that promotes inner healing, as well as harmony in all of our relationships and activities. Simply stated, meditation can help us create a new life.

The following pages will present many different types of meditations drawn from a wide range of religious and spiritual traditions. These include guided meditations, meditating on sacred symbols (such as mandalas), meditating to music, chanting, Zazen meditation, walking meditations, color meditations, "grounding" meditations, writing meditations, Tantric meditation, group meditations, and healing

6

meditations. We will also explore meditating in nature, especially with flowers, flowing water and trees. In addition to a short description of the meditation technique, we will offer clear how-to instructions.

Cautions Regarding Meditation

Just as water is essential for our physical well being, meditation is essential for our mental and spiritual well being. Yet if we drink water too quickly, or if we consume water in excess, it can be harmful to our health. By the same token, we can only derive maximum benefit from meditation if it is practiced appropriately and with care. The following are some "rules of the road" for prospective meditators:

1. The desire to meditate should be based on good intentions as opposed to developing mental, emotional or psychic power to wield over others. Psychic power, especially, needs to evolve naturally through self-awareness and selfless service.

2. Because meditation challenges old emotional and mental patterns, an open-minded attitude is essential from the start. Otherwise, meditation can actually reinforce negative habits.

3. If meditation practice is too intense over a long period of time, insomnia, irritability, and emotional instability can result. This can be due to excessive breathing exercises, meditation sessions that are too long, or the overuse of mantras.

4. The insights one gains through meditation need to be *real*. Ask: "How can this truth be expressed in my practical life?"

5. Meditation can make us more aware of our faults. We need to avoid indulging in negative self-judgments and focus instead of acknowledgment and transformation.

6. Meditation is not recommended for young children, and only for teenagers who genuinely feel attracted to it. However, relaxation exercises, simple breathing exercises, hatha yoga and t'ai chi help young people to become centered and "grounded."

7. Do not meditate (or stop meditating) if:

> -you feel tired
> -you feel nervous
> -you are having digestive problems
> -you have a headache
> -you have taken drugs or alcohol
> -you feel aggressive or critical towards others
> -you are becoming forgetful
> -you feel that you are being forced to meditate

Although the meditations presented in the following section are safe when practiced correctly, appropriate advice will be given to assure success with each method. Some are geared more for beginners, while others are more appropriate for advanced meditators.

Foundations

Seasoned practitioners of meditation teach that there are four basic "pillars" that can help support our daily meditation practice. They have to do with:

1. creating a sacred environment
2. choosing an appropriate meditation posture
3. learning how to relax
4. learning how to breathe

By paying attention to these four elements, we can greatly enhance our meditation experience.

1. Creating Sacred Space

Although one can meditate anywhere at any time of the day or night, those of us who have the opportunity to meditate at home can create an environment that will help us get the most out of this practice.

Quiet

First, find a place that is quiet. Those with lots of space can devote an entire room to meditation, using it exclusively for that purpose. Decorating the room with a think carpet, white or light-colored walls, and good ventilation, along with a simple chair or meditation cushions or mats to sit on will help create a comfortable environment conducive to meditation.

You may also wish to place sacred objects in the

room, such as portraits of spiritual teachers, a cross or a Jewish star, a statue or drawing of the Buddha or other religious item. Many people include fresh flowers and crystals. The idea is to create a space that will uplift your spirits: a type of personal sanctuary that is apart from the workaday world.

If you do not have the space to create a meditation room, the next-best choice is to use a study, a den or other room in the home where you can be apart from the rest of the household for thirty minutes at a time. A friend locks herself in a bathroom to meditate because it is the quietest place in the house.

The Home Altar

Creating an altar in your home is a very personal undertaking. The altar exists to remind you of your inner life whenever you see it. It also can serve as a centerpiece for your meditation practice or when you recite your daily prayers.

You can create your altar on a small table, or even on a shelf in the den, but it should be located where you can visit regularly and in private, often away from the most frequented areas of your home. Decorating the altar depends on your personal taste, and should reflect what *you* want rather than what *you* think is appropriate for an altar. The altar can contain a simple cloth covering, onto which you could place one or more votive candles, a religious symbol, a statue or picture of one or more saints or spiritual teachers, an incense holder, prayer beads or crystals. Fresh flowers add to the beauty and spiritual presence of any home altar and should be replaced regularly. Some people create an altar from empty space in a cluttered room, which sets it apart from the rest of the home.

Whatever type of altar you choose to create, it should only include elements that are personally important to you. Your altar is a sacred place in your home and a focal point to help you commune with the spiritual realms. For this reason, it should always be kept clean and free from other elements, such as dirt, dust, papers, books or anything else that is not intended to be part of the altar.

Over time, your altar can become a veritable "power spot" in your home. Like an electrical generator, the altar can be a repository of all of your feelings of devotion, compassion and positive intent: a continual source of positive energy in your home for the benefit of all who reside or visit there.

Incense

Incense has been traditionally used not only to eliminate odors, but to clean the subtle energies of the room. It is also believed to uplift the spirit. Some of the best is made at the international headquarters of The Theosophical Society in Chennai, India (available online and at Quest bookshops and Theosophical bookshops all over the world) and the "Auroshikha Agarbathies" incense made by the Sri Aurobindo Ashram in Pondicherry, India (available in many metaphysical bookstores and online).

Usually, incense made at a spiritual center is made with more care and greater consciousness than incense made in a ordinary factory. It is always a good idea to bless the incense before using it in any case, since it was probably handled by quite a few people before you purchased it.

11

Many different kinds of incense are available, and you need to choose the type of incense that is most compatible with your needs. If you are studying meditation with a teacher, he or she will be able to recommend a particular type that is best for you. If you are choosing your own incense, the following guide may be helpful.

Rose opens one's heart and awakens love.

Lavender stimulates the yin and yang balance; it steadies and calms the emotions.

Jasmine enhances our self-image and promotes confidence. Lotus inspires the desire to meditate; it also helps us to develop trust and receptivity in our relationships.

Patchouli awakens the desire for transformation; it helps increase our energy level.

Sandalwood stimulates the intuitive senses; awakens in us the desire to merge with the Divine within.

Frankincense inspires spiritual recognition; it elevates the mind and the emotions.

Myrrh strengthens endurance; it helps preserve youthful innocence.

Musk stimulates ones' primal instincts and helps draw a sexual partner to us. This incense may not be suitable for meditation.

Saffron awakens us to the Joy of the Gods; it is sometimes used in Tantra yoga and other forms of sexual ritual and devotion.

Gardenia is believed to assist in the opening of our energy centers or *chakras*.

Olive arouses passion and bonding; it develops grounded sensuality.

Almond helps to rekindle an awareness of sexual mysteries.

Coconut arouses desire for the exotic and in opening ourselves to new horizons; it is said to help bring out deep inner feelings.

As an alternative to incense, you can use aromatic oils to eliminate room odors and cleanse the subtle atmosphere of a room. Add several drops of mint, pine or eucalyptus oil to a glass of water and place the water near where you practice meditation.

Creating an Outdoor Altar

For those who have a quiet back yard, an outdoor altar can be a source of serenity and strength to be enjoyed during the warmer months of the year, or all year round if you live in a warm or temperate climate.

The creation of an altar will, of course, vary according to your personal taste. Some erect a small religious statue surrounded by a protective structure, while others prefer the statue or religious object to be exposed to the elements. The altar is often surrounded by flowers and decorative shrubbery, such as ornamental conifers or flowering plants like roses.

A Tree Shrine

In many cases, a tree on your property can become a tree shrine. Many of us instinctually feel that certain trees express a powerful energy with a special "keynote" quality, like protection, healing, wisdom or inspiration. The emotional and spiritual links between a human and a tree shrine can be quite profound. If a person is sufficiently open and sensitive, visiting a tree shrine can be a religious experience, which may assist in healing or personal transformation.

Selecting a tree to use as a tree shrine is a simple matter. If your property contains lots of trees, intuitively search out the tree towards which you feel the closest bond. Or you may decide to choose a tree by its secluded location. In Thailand, Buddhist monks designate a sacred tree by trying an orange ribbon around its trunk. Some people attach religious items to the tree, such as a cross, a statue of Buddha or image of a saint. The tree becomes a type of altar under which you can meditate and pray when the weather is good.

A tree shrine can be a friend for a lifetime. By developing a close relationship with a tree, we deepen our connection and love for the Earth. As a result, we can grow wiser and more sensitive to the life around us. We can also learn how to be more effective in serving as "earth stewards" who assist in the protection and healing of our planetary home. A tree shrine does not have to be planted. Many of them are already here, and merely have to be acknowledged.

14

Like the altar in a room in your home, an outdoor altar or tree shrine should be kept clean and well-maintained, and should not be used for purposes that are not directly related to your spiritual practice.

No Rushing

The place inside or outside your home that becomes your sacred meditation space will be the primary space (or one of the primary places) where you will engage in meditation. After you mediate, do not immediately get up and begin your daily tasks. Try to linger for a few moments in receptive silence in the sacred space which you have created. This may be followed by quietly doing some simple tasks around the home or garden in a meditative spirit, which will serve as a "living bridge" between your meditation practice and more mundane responsibilities and tasks.

2. Meditation Postures

There are numerous postures that people use when they meditate. Some are better designed for Westerners than others are. While a full lotus posture described later may be appropriate for an Indian *saddhu* or holy person, it may be extremely difficult (let alone uncomfortable) for a stressed-out middle-aged executive who is exploring meditation for the first time. Some postures involve sitting on the floor or on a meditation mat, while others call for sitting in a chair or lying on a mat or on the floor.

No matter what type of posture you choose, some general guidelines may be useful:

15

Your back and neck should be reasonably straight, resulting in what some meditators call a "dignified" posture. The inner organs (especially the stomach, lungs and intestines) should be free from pressure. If you feel that your shirt and pants are tight, release the top button.

Some people meditate in comfortable Indian-style or Japanese clothing that fits loosely on the body and does not bind the internal organs in any way. Others prefer to wear a jogging suit or sweat pants and a t-shirt.

During meditation, your blood should circulate unimpeded. If your legs tend to fall asleep during meditation, the discomfort will disrupt your practice. It may also make it impossible to get up when you are finished!

In a Chair or on the Floor?

You may feel comfortable sitting cross-legged on a cushion or a mat. There are also special "meditation chairs" sold in metaphysical book and supply stores and on the Internet that support your back. Many Westerners prefer to meditate in a simple, straight-backed chair that is neither too spartan nor overly-comfortable. Attempting to meditate in an overstuffed lounge chair or on a very comfortable sofa often leads to drowsiness or sleep.

Meditating in a Chair

Sit in a comfortable chair, feet placed firmly on the floor, with knees comfortably straight. This helps balance your body and keeps it free from tension.

Place your hands on your knees or thighs either facing either up or down. You could also place your left hand on your lap facing up, and place your right hand, also palm up, on top of it. With the palms facing up, you may also intertwine your fingers and place them on your lap; another recommended hand position would be to place your hands on your thighs, palms facing up. Gently place your thumb between the tips of your index and middle fingers.

The Half-Lotus

The half-lotus posture involves sitting cross legged on the floor or on a mat or cushion. Place your right foot gently on your left thigh. Be sure to keep your left foot on the floor under your right thigh. You may want to reposition yourself until you are comfortable. Place your hands, palms up, on your thigh, either open or with your thumb between the tips of your index and middle fingers.

The Full Lotus

As in the half-lotus, you sit on the floor, preferably atop a meditation mat or thin cushion. Gently place your right foot on your left thigh and your left foot on your right thigh. Newcomers to meditation often find this position impossible to achieve, so don't feel badly if you have trouble with it, especially at first.

One of the goals in meditation is to feel comfortable. While your ability to achieve the full lotus posture may well be an indicator of a flexible body, it is not necessarily a sign of advanced spirituality!

17

The Half Lotus

The Full Lotus

Kneeling

In this posture, you kneel on the meditation cushion with feet together, and place your weight on your knees. Whatever posture you choose, be aware of your body or head leaning forward or to the side. Gently correct your posture so that your spine is comfortably straight, with your head resting naturally atop your spine.

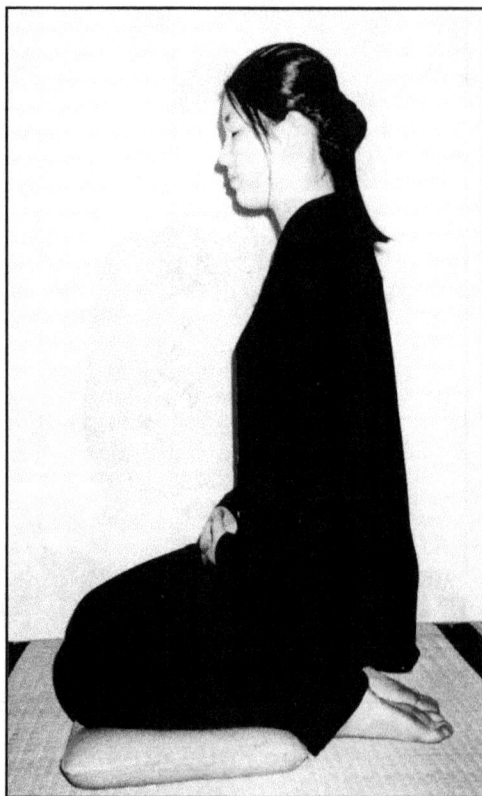

Kneeling

More about Meditation

Many people choose to close their eyes during meditation. You can also close your mouth and breathe through your nose, if you want. Place the tip of your tongue gently on the roof of your mouth behind the front teeth.

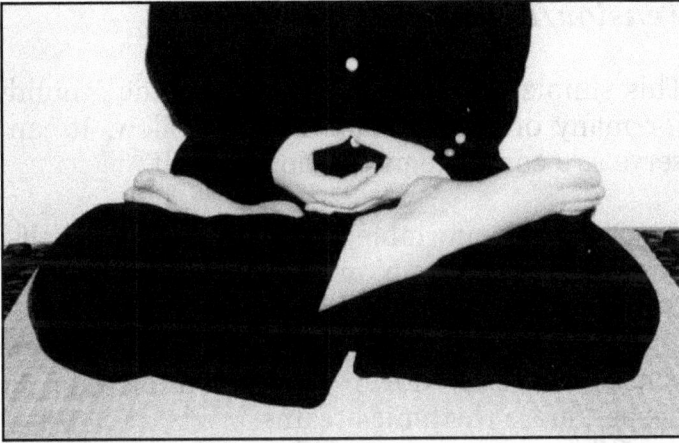

Position of the Hands

There is no magic period of time for meditation. Begin meditating for five to ten minutes, and gradually increase the length of your meditation session over time to twenty or thirty minutes. Experienced meditators are able to remain in a posture for three hours or more. When you are ready to rise after concluding your meditation, do so gently. If you feel stiffness or pain anywhere in your body, massage that area gently until it feels better. Get up slowly and gently, with dignity.

3. Basic Relaxation Exercises

The following exercises help you to relax. When you begin any of the meditations described in this book, you may want to try one or more of these simple methods, or take elements from these exercises that you feel work for you the best.

21

Tension/Release Exercise

This simple technique can either lay the groundwork for many of the meditations that follow. It can also serve as a complete meditation in itself.

Sit in a comfortable position, either in a half-lotus posture on a cushion or seated upright in a comfortable straight-backed chair.

Become aware of your breathing. Begin to consciously slow down your breathing rate, taking deeper, more rhythmic breaths.

When you exhale, say the word "peace" out loud, or use another word with peaceful connotations, such as *shanti* or *shalom*. A goal in breath rate would be a count of six as you inhale, and a count of six when you exhale.

Be aware of any tension in your body. Silently scan your face, neck, shoulders, chest, arms, hands, stomach, pelvis, legs and feet to perceive any areas of tension. If you come upon an area that is tense, focus your calming breath to that area.

When you inhale, visualize the breath moving towards the tense area, bathing it with warmth and calming energy. As you exhale, visualize the tension leaving that part of your body. Continue this process until your body is completely relaxed.

Progressive Relaxation Exercise (1)

Sit comfortably in a chair, or in a cross-legged position on a bed or on the floor. First, tense the muscles in your face, and hold this tension for a few seconds. Then completely relax.

Now gradually move down your neck and tense the muscles. The completely relax.

Repeat this exercise in different sections of the body by working down through the shoulders, arms, chest, stomach, buttocks, anus, thighs, calves and feet. By the time you reach your feet, will almost surely be in a relaxed state.

As a variation, you can tense all the muscles of the body and then relax them all at the same time. You could also tense a particular muscle and then relax and gently massage it.

When you release tension, you can let your breath out, accompanied by a long "aaahh" or a sigh. This will allow you get in touch with your deeper feelings and help you release them.

Quiet, deep breathing can follow this exercise.

Progressive Relaxation Exercise (2)

Sit in a comfortable position, either in a straight-backed chair or on a meditation cushion placed on the floor.

Close your eyes and focus on your breath. Take full and easy breaths. As you inhale, feel life-giving oxygen flow into your lungs. As you exhale, feel your body relax. With each exhalation you feel your body relax more and more. Feel your shoulders relax, your buttocks relax, your legs and feet relax, your belly relax, your arms and hands relax, your head and face and jaw relax. Tension is progressively leaving your body, and will continue to do so throughout this exercise.

Feel your mind release as well. As it relaxes, imagine that your mind is becoming more open, more

23

alert and more free.

Slowly let go of any anxieties, emotional tension, and fears with each exhalation of your breath. Feel yourself becoming emotionally relaxed as you exhale. Say to yourself: "I am relaxing." Continue this process for five minutes, or until you reach a level of deep relaxation.

4. Breathing

Although all of us breathe, we usually view the rhythm of our breathing as automatic. We are often not aware of the quality of our breathing and tend to take partial, shallow breaths using only the upper part of the lungs. We often hold our breath or take shallow, quick breaths (especially when we are tense, fearful or nervous) without being conscious of it.

Try the following simple breathing exercise:

Consciously take a few short, shallow and irregular breaths. Be aware of how you feel. Chances are, you will feel anxious, uneasy and ungrounded.

Now take a few deep, full breaths, counting to six at each inhalation and counting to six as you exhale. Chances are that this deeper, slower breathing helps you feel more calm and comfortable.

When rapid, shallow breathing becomes habitual or chronic, we limit the amount of air that we take into our body. This not only impairs our body's ability to oxygenate the blood and other vital tissues, but it often makes us feel nervous, mentally sluggish and tired.

In contrast, deep, rhythmic breathing is essential for proper oxygenation, and can have a positive impact on how we feel mentally and emotionally. On the following pages, we'll offer a number of simple breathing techniques that promote both relaxation and vitality.

The Awareness Breath

Sit in a comfortable position. Gently inhale while you do a slow count to four (approximately 4 seconds), hold your breath quietly for a count of two and then slowly exhale for a count of four.

As you breathe, pay attention to your breath. Your mind will probably begin to wander. Simply be aware of this and gently bring yourself back to paying attention to your breath. By constantly directing your thought back to your breath, you are building a "muscle" of attentiveness and one-pointedness that will help you in your daily activities.

The Counting Breath

With practice, the following breathing method will enable you to relax whenever you feel nervous or anxious. It can be performed at any place and at any time. Moreover, it can also lay the foundation for meditation practice.

Sit in a comfortable position. Gently inhale while you do a slow count to four (approximately 4 seconds), hold your breath quietly for a count of two and then slowly exhale for a count of four. You can easily extend this breathing for a longer period, counting to six or even eight, while holding your breath for a count of four. Remember that such breaths should never be forced or uncomfortable to you. Breathe with awareness, and feel the life-giving oxygen being drawn into your body. As you exhale, imagine your body being cleansed.

Sitting comfortably, as you inhale, count "One, one, one, one..." and count "Two, two, two, two..." as you exhale slowly. Then count "Three, three, three, three..." as you slowly fill your lungs again with air. Continue this process up to the count up to ten, and then begin from "one" once more.

As you inhale, count slowly up to ten, and then count from one to ten as you exhale. Repeat this process as many times as you need in order to fully concentrate on your breathing.

Another method involves counting "one" while you inhale *and* while you exhale, so that each complete breath counts as one number. After a complete inhalation and exhalation, you begin again and count "two," until you complete your second full breath. Continue to count your breaths up to the number "ten" and then begin again from "one."

The Standing Breath

Stand comfortably with your spine straight, your knees slightly bent, inhaling slowly and deeply through your nose. Make sure that you are breathing into your abdomen rather than the chest: place your hand on your belly to feel the air expand it as you inhale; gently pull in your stomach muscles as you exhale.

As you inhale, imagine in your mind's eye that you are surrounded by a brilliant golden light that is flowing into your body towards your abdomen and onwards through the rest of your body, including your hands and feet. After inhaling, hold your breath and count slowly to three with each count standing for one second. (With practice, you can hold your breath for up to ten seconds). Slowly exhale through your mouth, feeling any tensions in your body melt away. Yawn and stretch. Repeat this exercise three times.

The Yogi Complete Breath

Learning how to breathe in a way that involves both the upper and lower parts of the lungs has been viewed as vital by yogis for centuries. Perhaps one of the most important breath techniques to learn is known as "The Yogi Complete Breath" first introduced to the West by Yogi Ramacharaka (believed to be the pseudonym of the author and leader of the New Thought movement, William Walker Atkinson) in the early part of the 20th century. He described performing this breath as follows:

1. Stand or sit erect.

2. Breathing through the nostrils, inhale steadily, first filling the lower part of the lungs, which is accompanied by bringing into play the diaphragm, while [distending] exerts a gentle pressure on the abdominal organs, pushing forward the front walls of the abdomen.

3. Then fill the middle part of the lungs, pushing out the lower ribs, breastbone and chest.

4. Then fill the higher portion of the lungs, protruding the upper chest, thus lifting the chest, including the

upper six or seven pairs of ribs.

5. In the final movement, the lower part of the abdomen will be slightly drawn in, which movement gives the lungs a support and also helps to fill the highest part of the lungs.

In *The Science of Breath*, Yogi Ramacharaka reminds us that this breath does not consist of three distinct movements, but is rather one continuous, fluid movement. He recommends that we retain this breath for a couple of seconds and then exhale slowly, drawing in the abdomen slightly as the air leaves the lungs, and relaxing the chest and abdomen after the air is released.

You can do the Yogi Complete Breath whenever you feel like it, though at first you may want to do this breath during a period of quiet contemplation, or just before beginning your daily meditation. Gradually, you can begin consciously breathing fully and deeply in more and more of your daily activities, until deep, rhythmic breathing becomes a normal part of your life.

Only living people breathe. Dead people don't. The more we breathe, the more alive we are. And the more we practice deep, rhythmic breathing, the more we partake of oxygen: the essence of life itself.

5. Keeping a Journal

While not considered an essential part of meditation, writing your experiences in a journal can be helpful for anyone interested in meditation. On one hand, the journal can help remind you of your actual experience with different meditation techniques, thus allowing you to improve your techniques. It also helps you to enjoy deeper insights in yourself: what makes you impatient, how you breathe, what areas in your body cause you difficulty.

Finally, the journal is an excellent place for you to record valuable impressions, ideas and insights that may have come to you during your meditation practice. When left to memory alone, much valuable information can be lost. Your journal allows you to maintain a permanent record of your insights and experiences, which you can refer to easily.

The way that you maintain a journal is entirely up to you. However, some meditators record the date, time, and subject of the meditation, with additional sections devoted to realizations and difficulties that come up during the meditation. The following sample journal entry is included as an example:

Date: January 25
Time: 8-8:20 AM
Subject: candle meditation
Difficulties: I lost track of my breathing during the relaxation exercise, and had to return to it several times. It was difficult to relax at first. While looking at the candle, I spaced out a few times.
Realizations: I never realized how beautiful a candle can be. I felt inspired and calmed by the flame. I want to burn candles at the table when I have dinner with my husband. So romantic!

Meditations

Alignment Meditation

One of the goals of meditation is to align our thoughts and emotions with our deepest essence or "core." There are many different ways to do this. The following method is but one of many possibilities, and can easily be modified according to your personal needs and goals.

1. Find a comfortable place where you can be quiet and alone.

2. Select a comfortable position - sitting in a chair or cross-legged on a cushion or rug. If you are outdoors, you may wish to lean against a tree or lie down on the ground.

3. Practice one of the Basic Relaxation Exercises described earlier.

4. If you prefer to meditate with your eyes open, select something simple to focus your eyes upon, like a candle, a flower, a religious symbol or other beautiful object. This will help prevent your mind from wandering. If you keep your eyes closed, try to visualize a field of pure, white light.

5. Begin to breathe slowly and deeply, becoming aware of your breath as it enters and leaves your body. Each time your mind wanders to other thoughts or is disturbed by outside noises, gently bring your

attention back to the easy, natural rhythm of your breathing. If you have trouble keeping your mind on your breath, count each inhalation and exhalation up to ten, and then start over again.

6. As you relax physically, you may find that various feelings come and go. Don't repress them. Calmly observing them may cause them to gradually lose their intensity.

7. Gradually intuit and then visualize the concept of oneness with all beings. Express your desire to experience the reality of oneness as an integral part of your life today, either in silence or out loud: "I pray to realize my oneness with nature today."

8. Repeat this visualization slowly several times. You can also express other desires or yearnings you have which you want to integrate into your life during the day. This process is akin to "sending a letter of intent to the universe."

9. After having expressed your keynote visualization, relax and be receptive once more. Continue your relaxed, deep breathing for at least three minutes and feel the sense of oneness living inside your body, near the heart. Feel it streaming out into the room, into the neighborhood, and further out into the world. Complete your meditation gradually and in silence.

Rachel's Meditation Technique

The following simple meditation technique is practiced regularly by one of my oldest and dearest friends. It is being shared in her own words.

I sit in a chair and concentrate on my breathing, both feeling it and "hearing" it with an inner ear; it helps me to concentrate.

I count my breaths from one to ten, and then start over again. When I get distracted, I get back to the counting.

There are variations to this method. I may visualize white light, and the imagery of a mountain that is unshakeable in storms and other types of weather.

I also play with how to hold my hands. Usually, my hands are in a "palm up" position, open and with thumbs touching.

I meditate every day, from 20 to 30 minutes in the morning before I do other things when the house is quiet.

Zazen Meditation

Zazen, or "sitting meditation" places emphasis on direct seeing through sitting quietly and not thinking. As an aspect of Zen Buddhism, Zazen is known as *Ch'an* meditation in China. The following meditation method is based on the teachings of the Japanese Zen master Dogen Zenji.

Place

As with other meditation practices, Zazen should be done in a quiet place where you can meditate without disturbances. The room should be neither too dark nor too bright, warm in winter and cool in summer, and should be kept clean. Ideally, this space should contain a picture or statue of the Buddha. Fresh flowers and incense should be placed in front of the image.

Preparing for Meditation: Five Suggestions

When doing Zazen, meditation instructors offer the following guidelines:

1. Do not meditate if you haven't had sufficient sleep or when you are very tired.
2. Avoid overeating and excessive alcohol before sitting.
3. Wash your hands and face before sitting.
4. Clean, loose fitting garments should be worn.
5. Place a thick mat (known in Japan as a *zabuton*) in front of the wall and place a cushion (*zafu*) on top of it. Sit cross-legged on the zafu, placing the base of your spine at the center so that half of the zafu is behind you. Rest your knees firmly on the zabuton.

Body Position

If possible, try to sit in the full lotus position described earlier, known in Japanese as *kekkafuza*. If this is too difficult, try to sit in the half-lotus position, known as *hankafuza*. In either of these positions, both knees can be rested on the zabuton.

Posture

Straighten the lower part of your back, push your buttocks outward and push your hips forward. Straighten your spine, but not so that you feel uncomfortable.

Pull in your chin and extend your neck as though reaching to the ceiling. Your ears should be parallel to your shoulders. Your nose should be in line with your navel. After straightening your back, relax your shoulders, back and abdomen without changing your posture. Sit up straight, leaning neither to the right nor left, neither forward nor backward.

Position of Hands

Moving your hands near your lap, place the right hand (palm up) on your left foot, and your left hand on your right palm. The tips of your thumbs should lightly touch each other, This position is called Cosmic Mudra or *hokkaijoin*. Place the tips of your thumbs in front of your navel, with your arms held slightly apart from your body. If you aren't wearing traditional monk's robes, place a towel on your lap, so that the Cosmic Mudra position can be easily maintained.

The Mouth

In Zazen, the mouth is kept closed. Place your tongue lightly against the roof of your mouth.

The Eyes

Zen masters recommend that you keep your eyes slightly open, with your vision cast down at about a 45-degree angle in front of you. Without focusing on anything in particular, allow your field of vision to encompass everything in front of you. If your eyes are closed, it is easier to daydream or become drowsy.

Breathing

Begin your breathing by quietly making a deep exhalation and inhalation. Then open your mouth slightly and exhale slowly and smoothly. In order to expel all the air from your lungs, exhale from your abdomen, pulling the abdomen in slowly. Then close your mouth and inhale through your nose naturally. This form of breathing is known in Japanese as *kanki-issoku.*

Generally speaking, continue doing abdominal breathing through your nose during meditation. Do not try to control your breathing, but allow it to happen naturally. Allow your long breaths to be even and long, and short breaths to be short; strive to become aware of the difference. Your breathing should be so quiet that others cannot hear you. Beginners may wish to count their breaths, which increases awareness and helps regulate breathing.

Swaying the Body

When you feel the need, swaying the body can be a part of Zazen meditation. Place your hands palms-up on your knees and gently sway the upper part of your body from the left to the right. This can be done several times. Without moving your hips, move your trunk as though it were a long, flexible pole leaning to the right and the left, so that you stretch the hip muscles. You may also sway forward and backward.

As you sway, each movement becomes smaller and smaller until if ceases with your body in an upright position. This exercise should take several minutes. At this point, assume the Cosmic Mudra with your hands once more.

Awareness

During meditation, do not concentrate on any particular subject or attempt to control your thinking. By maintaining proper posture and as your breathing settles down, your mind will become quiet as well.

If thoughts come up, do not struggle with them nor try to escape from them. Simply leave them alone, and allow them to come and go freely. The goal here is to awaken from distraction or drowsiness and return to the correct posture and breathing moment by moment.

Completing Zazen

When you finish Zazen, bow, place your hands palms up on your thighs, and gently sway your body (left to right and forwards and backwards) a few times. Then sway a bit more extensively, so that you actually feel your muscles stretching. Take a deep breath. Slowly unfold your legs. Stand up slowly and carefully, especially if your legs are asleep.

Thought Meditation

One of the primary purposes of meditation is to make us more aware of our thought processes. The following meditation exercise is designed to assist in this process of self-awareness.

1. Do one the Basic Relaxation Exercises described earlier.

2. As you breathe, be aware of each thought as it comes up, without censuring it, resisting it, or judging it in any way. Try to observe the connection of one thought to the other (if any). Watch each thought as it departs, and be aware of the next thought that comes up. Continue this process of active observation for three to five minutes.

3. You will probably find a combination of present-day concerns, old memories, odd associations and projections for the future. Record them in a notebook, describing them as you saw them. Write down everything you can remember.

4. If you continue this meditation for several days or weeks, review your notes from time to time, comparing the thoughts that come up each day during your practice.

Empty Space Meditation

In the previous meditation exercise, you have observed your thoughts as they came up. The following meditation exercise is similar, yet it helps us focus on the concept of *empty space* that exists between thoughts.

1. Do one of the Basic Relaxation Exercises described earlier.

2. As in the previous meditation, be aware of each thought as it comes up, without criticising it, resisting it, or judging it in any way. Try to observe the connection of one thought to the other (if any). Watch each thought as it departs, and be aware of the next thought that comes up.

3. Be aware of any *space between thoughts*: moments of quiet, calm or emptiness that may be found between your thoughts. Be aware of them without trying to shorten or lengthen them in any way. With practice, these moments of "sacred space" will enlarge.

Meditation for Mind Expansion

1. Sit in a quiet place. Devote several minutes to one of the relaxation techniques described earlier.

2. When you feel sufficiently relaxed and centered, read a spiritual or other thought-provoking statement. Some possible statements include:

Let the kingdom of your heart be so wide that no one is excluded. -*N. Sri Ram.*

He who does not attempt to make peace when small discords arise, is like a bee's hive which leaks drops of honey. Soon, the whole hive collapses. - *Nagarjuna*

People ought not to consider so much what they are to do as what they *are*; let them *be* good and their ways and deeds will shine brightly. -*Meister Eckhart*

The key to humanity's trouble... has been to take and not give, to accept and not share, to grasp and not to distribute. -*Alice A. Bailey*

It is in the heart center that our inner nature grows to fullness. Once the heart center opens, all blockages dissolve, and a spirit of intuition spreads throughout our entire body so that our whole being comes alive. - *Tarthang Tulku*

   3. Devote several minutes *thinking* about the idea and explore its meanings.
   4. At the same time, open yourself to inspiration and understanding regarding this idea. At this point, your mind is more alive and expansive, opening itself to new possibilities and ways of perception.
   5. Close your eyes and continue to observe your thoughts, being aware of any wandering or unrelated thinking. Gently bring your consciousness back to the concept at hand.
   6. After several minutes, take several deep breaths and conclude your meditation.

Candle Meditation

Fire is one of the primary forces of the universe, and has always been worshiped as a medium of prophecy and as a means inspire. In earlier times, meditating on a burning a candle was believed to help one connect with the spirit within. Not only is a candle aesthetically pleasing, but it is a constant source of comfort, especially if we are feeling lonely, upset or depressed.

1. Sit in a comfortable position, either in a straight-backed chair or on a cushion on the floor. Place a new white candle in front of you and light it.

2. Perform one of the Basic Relaxation exercises described earlier, paying special attention to your breathing.

3. As you breathe, observe the lighted candle as a symbol of hope and life.

4. If your thoughts wander, try not to follow their trail. Gently bring your mind back to the flame.

5. After ten or more minutes, conclude your meditation and extinguish the candle.

Meditations on Sacred Symbols

Sacred symbols express a meaning without words. Many, such as the cross, star or swastika, are specific to certain ancient religions and cultures, while others, like a lighted candle, have universal meanings. Many symbols will have specific meanings to each individual; a devout Christian will have a very different impression of a cross than would an observant Jew. However, when doing this meditation, try to move past any preconceived ideas you may have about a particular symbol.

1. After doing one of the Basic Relaxation Exercises, choose a sacred symbol on which to meditate. You can either use a picture of a symbol, or visualize the symbol in your mind's eye. Before choosing a sacred symbol, you may want to spend a little time studying its sacred meanings. Some suggested symbols to meditate on and their thumbnail meanings include:

Cross: eternal life; union of spirit and matter (Figure 5).

The Symbol of Change from the I Ching (Figure 6).

Star of David: the unity of the masculine and feminine aspects of nature (Figure 7).

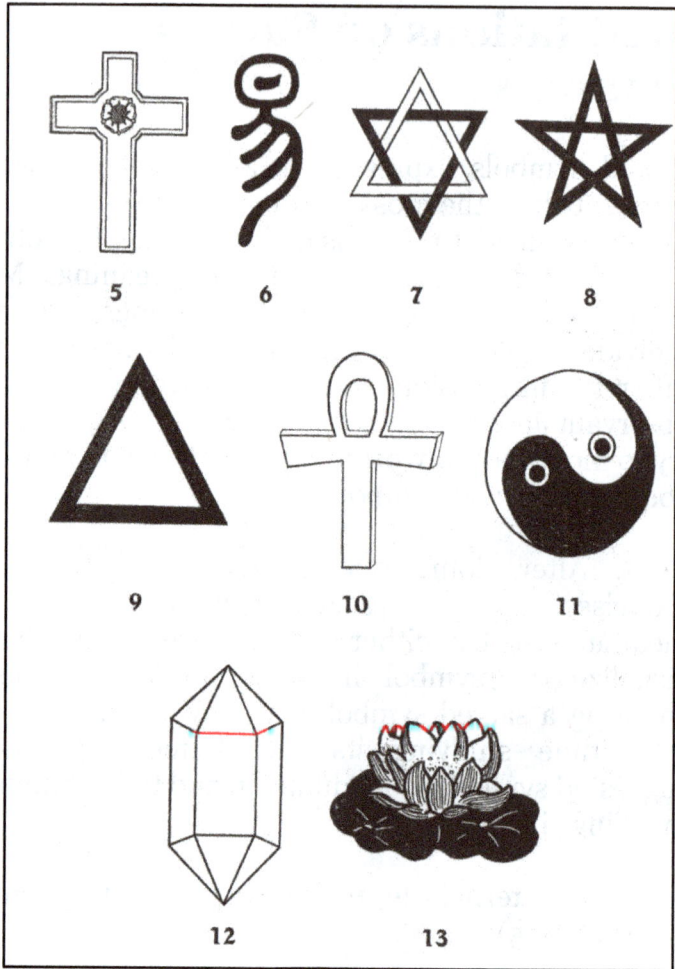

Sacred Symbols

Five-pointed Star: a symbol of humanity (Figure 8).

Triangle: the Trinity: father, son and spirit;

upper part: one life; two sides: duality of existence; base: offspring of spirit and matter (Figure 9).

Crescent: the moon; emblem of Isis, the Egyptian earth goddess.

Ankh: immortality; the primordial movement and state of cosmic being (Figure 10).

Yin-Yang: dynamic balance between the masculine and feminine (Figure 11).

Spiral: action in ascending spirit.

Disc: the cosmic egg; the entire cosmic process by which worlds and living beings are born.

Vertical line: spirit, Godhead

Horizontal line: matter; Earth

Diamond: the many facets of Divine-wisdom (Figure 12)

Snake: wisdom.

Lotus: a universal symbol; creation and spiritual realization (Figure 13).

Tree: being grounded in the earth, with one's branches reaching towards heaven.

2. Devote between five to ten minutes to the sacred symbol, allowing your mind to ponder its structure, form and meaning; chances are that new and unexpected ideas and impressions will come into your mind. If you wish, you can later record your impressions in your journal.

3. As you conclude your meditation, take several deep breaths and stretch your body. Slowly rise from your meditation posture.

Word Symbol Meditation

Words have power, and contain the ability to teach, inspire, harm or heal. The following meditation is designed to help us to more deeply understand the power of certain words and feel their creative power.

After performing one of the Basic Relaxation Exercises, select an index card on which you have clearly written a word in blue or violet-colored ink.

As you watch your breathing, place the card before you and spend several minutes pondering the word.

Ask yourself the following questions: "What does this word mean to me?" "What associations (if any) does it bring up?" "How does the word affect me emotionally, mentally or spiritually?"

Continue to be aware of your breathing, and slowly come out of your meditation. Devote several more minutes to recording your impressions in a journal. You may wish to meditate on a different word each day, or devote several meditations to one specific

word of your choice. Some suggested words on which
to meditate include:

Light	Right Speech
Peace	Right Thought
Hope	Right Action
Love	Discrimination
Love Wisdom	Detachment
Guru or Teacher	Healing
Surrender	Wholeness
Movement	Courage
Compassion	Integration
Humility	Spontaneity
Truthfulness	Relinquishment
Trust	Eternal
Trustworthiness	Beauty
Patience	Holy
Responsibility	Creativity
God	Harmony
Universal	Inclusiveness

Meditating to Music

Music is a powerful form of energy that can help us enter new and different states of consciousness. On the physical level, music has been shown to cause changes in breathing, muscular tension, heartbeat and blood pressure.

Many of us have found that music often affects us emotionally: it can sooth, inspire, or make us sad or depressed. Harmonious music in particular can create vibratory patterns in our consciousness, and perhaps help us achieve greater harmony in ourselves. Some types of music can increase the brain's alpha wave activity, often associated with meditative practice. This is one reason why music is frequently used as a prelude to meditation practice, although music can become the object of a meditation itself.

We can play a recording of quiet music as we perform one of the Basic Relaxation exercises before beginning our meditation.

We can also utilize music while we chant. Music from India or China are especially conducive to mantra meditation. Some recorded chants have music accompanying them, and we can simply "join in" as we listen.

We can also meditate to music, whether at home or at a concert.

Choosing a piece of classical, New Age, Indian sitar or other type of quiet restful music, perform one of the Basic Relaxation Exercises described earlier. After you are relaxed, listen to the musical piece without interruption for three minutes or more. As you pay attention to your breathing, be aware of the individual and collective sounds and their relationship to each other.

Take note of the harmony, the movement, and the entrance and exit of the various instruments. Be aware, too, of how the music makes you feel. While the music is playing, it may be easy to become lost in daydreams, so strive to be aware of any unrelated thoughts that may come up. If your mind wanders, gently return your focus to the music itself.

You may wish to devote three or four minutes to this meditation exercise at first, and gradually increase your practice to fifteen minutes or more.

Energy Meditations

The following two meditations are designed to enable you to safely access the energy of the Universe, known in the East as *chi* or *prāna*. Although best done in the morning, they can be performed whenever you feel the need for more energy during the course of the day.

Contacting Universal Energy

1. Seated comfortably in a straight-backed chair or on a cushion or mat, do one of the Basic Relaxation exercises described earlier.

2. Continue to pay attention to your breathing; close your eyes.

3. Visualize yourself flying upward like a soaring bird. Light is shining all around you. Feel the radiance and warmth of this dazzling, bright light. Feel this light flowing through you, bathing you with energy. This energy brings with it a sense of inner peace and

well being. Acknowledge that this light not only invigorates you, but guides you in making the correct choices in your life as well. Continue to be aware of your breathing.

4. After several minutes, visualize yourself descending back to earth again, yet continue to feel some of this bright light within you.

5. Open your eyes and slowly come out of your meditation.

With a brief expression of thanks, you are now ready to begin your day!

Illumination Meditation

1. Sit comfortably in a straight-backed chair or on a cushion or mat. Perform one of the Basic Relaxation exercises, being especially aware of your breathing.

2. Visualize your body and mind as being a dark-grey mass, totally devoid of light. Feel the heaviness, the emptiness and the lack of energy and inspiration. Allow this feeling to continue to a minute or two.

3. Now, imagine a tiny source of pure, white light beginning to shine within you. It can originate in the heart, at the base of your spine, in your brain, or any other part of your body.

4. Imagine this light growing in both size and brightness. Feel its warmth and its healing. See this light expand while it permeates your entire body with light, including your arms and legs, fingers and toes. As you breathe, see this light radiating outward, filling the atmosphere with its energy and warmth.

5. Now, mentally reduce the force until you feel

the core of light and its radiance filling your entire body.

6. Quietly conclude your meditation while retaining the feeling of being filled with light. Take a few deep breaths and stretch before getting up from your seated position.

The Four Facets of Loving

Understanding the meaning of love is one of life's great challenges. Since the beginning of human culture, poets, religious leaders and philosophers have written volumes about what it means to truly love.

Many agree that there are four important factors that allow love to thrive: compassion, understanding, freedom from judgment and listening. In fact, all of these aspects are intimately related, and together lay the groundwork for a positive self-image, successful relationships and a life of purpose and fulfillment.

You can focus on one quality each morning for four mornings, although you may want to repeat the four-day cycle regularly. It is also valuable to record your experiences in a journal. This will be useful to reflect on your life from time to time, and they can also serve as the foundation for your personal meditation themes in the future.

Sit in a comfortable posture, either in a straight-backed chair or on a cushion placed on the floor. Do one of the Basic Relaxation exercises described earlier in this book, or another relaxation method of your choice. Light a white candle if you wish to do so.

Compassion

1. Before you begin, you might pray or affirm "I wish to explore the meaning of compassion in my life today."

2. Pen and notebook in hand, ponder the elements of compassion. What does the word mean to you? How do people manifest compassion in life? Think of people you know who are in need (including some who may not be easy to deal with). Send them feelings of compassion at this time. How can you share compassion with people, animals and plants in your daily life? How can you show greater compassion towards yourself? Observe your thoughts and feelings as you explore these issues, without evaluating them or judging them in any way. Record them in your notebook.

3. After ten minutes, conclude your meditation.

Understanding

1. Before you begin, you can pray or affirm "I wish to explore the elements of understanding in my life today."

2. Pen and notebook in hand, ask yourself what are the elements of understanding? What facilitates them and what stops them from taking place? Who do I have trouble understanding in my life? For today, agree to place yourself in their situation and take on their point of view. Know that although you do not need to agree with them, the goal today is to deepen your level of *understanding*.

3. As in the previous meditation exercise, observe your thoughts and feelings as you explore these issues,

without evaluating them or judging them in any way. Be especially aware of any currents of justification and resistance you may have. Record your impressions in your notebook.

4. After ten minutes, conclude your meditation.

Freedom from Judgment

1. Before you begin, pray or affirm "I pray to explore my tendency to judge people and situations today."

2. Devote several minutes to exploring how you judge yourself, other people and situations in your life. Be specific, and record these instances in your journal. Ask yourself "What are the currents behind my judgmental attitude?" "How do I feel when I judge myself and others?" "How does judging destroy understanding and compassion?" Be aware of your thoughts and feelings as they come up, and record them in your journal.

3. Today, commit yourself to be aware of making judgments towards yourself, other people and situations you find yourself in today. Remember that it may be too early to "take a vacation" from making judgments; your goal today is to be aware of them and their ramifications in your relationships with others.

4. Conclude your meditation with a few deep breaths and stretches.

Listening

1. Before you begin, pray or affirm "I pray to understand the importance of listening."

2. Explore your reactions when others speak with

51

you. Do you think about a response before they finish talking to you? Do you hear their words but do not really listen to others? Do you interrupt them? Do you "tune out" when you hear things that make you uncomfortable or that you don't like? How do you feel when you do this? How do you feel when others do not listen to you? Cite specific instances with specific people. Write them down in your journal.

3. Ponder on the elements of what involves truly listening to others. Record them in your notebook.

4. Commit yourself to be aware of *not* listening when you converse with others today.

5. Conclude your meditation with several deep breaths and stretches.

The Eightfold Path Meditation

According to traditional Buddhist teachings, the way of liberation is "The Noble Eightfold Path." Less a religious doctrine than a form of moral psychology, the eight factors of the path include:

1. *Right understanding*, or knowledge of the true nature of existence.

2. *Right thought*, or thought that free from negativity, sensuality, ill-will and cruelty. Right thought also involves being aware of when we have wrong, inaccurate, divisive or destructive beliefs.

3. *Right speech*, calling for speech that is not only true, kind and helpful, but speech which does not

contain gossip, harshness, or idle chit-chat.

4. Right action, involving not just the avoidance of killing, stealing and adultery, but being involved in personal, political and social activities that heal, nourish and alleviate pain in the world.

5. Right livelihood, involving an occupation that does no harm to conscious living beings, but also a vocation or avocation that does good for society and benefits the earth.

6. Right effort, which involves not only cultivating wholesome qualities in ourselves, but getting involved in activities that benefit the welfare of other living beings.

7. Right mindfulness, which involves developing mental awareness and clarity; it also calls upon us to focus on ideas and concepts that are is important in life, as opposed to devoting one's thoughts to worry, trivia, or celebrity gossip.

8. Right concentration, calling for the cultivation of a mind that is both collected and focused through meditation.

The following meditation plan is designed to be used over a period of eight days. Each day will be devoted to meditating on one aspect of the Noble Eightfold Path.

For this meditation, you will need a notebook and a picture or other image of the Buddha. You may also wish to write down each aspect of the Eightfold Path on an index card refer to during meditation.

1. Seat yourself comfortably in a chair or on a cushion on the floor. Perform the Basic Relaxation Exercise, or another relaxation method of your choice. Be aware of your breathing, which should be deep, slow and even.

2. With the Buddha image before you, pray for clarity and enlightenment. This can be a short prayer like "I pray to open myself to the wisdom of the Noble Eightfold Path and learn to follow it in my daily life."

3. Choose an aspect of the Noble Eightfold Path and read the card that this aspect is written upon. Ponder the meaning and ramifications of this aspect carefully. Ask about the meaning of this aspect:

> To what extent do you manifest this aspect in your life? In what areas is your understanding and practice lacking? Be totally honest with yourself, allowing your thoughts to flow freely, writing them down in your notebook. At the same time, strive to be objective, being aware of feelings of pride, remorse or guilt that may come up. Devote five to ten minutes to this exercise.

4. When you are ready to conclude your meditation, take a few deep breaths. Express gratitude for your insights. Gently stretch your body as you slowly rise from your meditation posture.

Mantra Meditations

We live in a world of sound. Sound is essentially a form of energy that is transmitted through air and other conductors. Sounds can range from soothing sounds like the movement of the wind through the trees, the gurgling of a stream, or the breaking of waves on a rocky shore. Other pleasant sounds include the quiet ringing of bells.

Discordant sounds like rap music, the screeching of brakes or the incessant barking of a dog, tend to inhibit our ability to think clearly. Noise pollution affects us physically, emotionally and mentally, often producing stress and feelings of ungroundedness.

By the same token, human speech can also have a powerful impact in our daily life; we really know very little about how it affects us. Speech tones, volume and certain words are types of energy that make us react in different ways. In some cases, a hateful word or a careless phrase can hurt us even more than getting punched in the stomach.

The human voice has long played a role in religious practices throughout the world. Chanting, praying and singing are all powerful methods of using voice vibration and the power of sound to elevate our consciousness and make us more receptive to spiritual forces. Singing spiritual hymns, and chanting heartfelt prayers and the holy names of God have always been viewed as an essential part of daily spiritual practice.

The Prophet Mohammed counseled, "Say unto mankind: cry unto Allah or cry unto the Most Merciful, unto whichever we cry it is the same." The Buddha is believed to have said, "All who sincerely call upon my name will come to me after death, and I will take them to paradise."

Serious devotees of the spiritual life, from Catholic monks to Hindu yogis, Jewish Kabbalists, to Tibetan Buddhist monks, have a powerful tradition of chanting that has survived to this day.

The word *mantra* comes from the Sanskrit, meaning "the thought that liberates and protects." A mantra has been defined as "a combination of sacred syllables which forms a nucleus of spiritual energy" or "a sacred syllable or word or set of words through the repetition and reflection of which one attains perfection or realization of the Self."

Using a mantra in spiritual practice involves chanting, singing, or even humming a sacred sound that can either help prepare the foundation for meditation, or to elevate one's consciousness during meditation itself.

A mantra involves the repetition of the name of God, such as *Ave Maria* by the Christians or *Elohim* by the Jews. Chanting the name of Jesus has been a vital aspect of Christian meditation, while chanting the name of the goddess Oshoun or the god Oshalá has been practiced by adherents to African religions like Macumba and the Brazilian Candomblé and Umbanda. It can also involve repeating a sacred word like *shanti* or peace.

Aside from the vibration of the actual names or sacred words, a mantra can have powerful personal associations. For Muslims, there is no word more meaningful than Allah, while the word *Aum* or *Om* is viewed by the Hindus as symbolizing the essence of spiritual reality.

Yet one must beware of mechanically reciting a mantra or any sacred sound. The power of a mantra is proportionate to the feeling that we put into its expression. For this reason, our personal choice of a mantra is extremely important, and should ideally be a sacred word or name that we can personally relate to.

Having said this, many mantras are universal in scope. Based on the idea that there is no such thing as a "Jewish soul" or a Christian soul" but rather a "divine soul," the actual mantra is unimportant and that any sacred word or name can impart a powerful spiritual vibration and uplift the consciousness of any receptive individual.

Reciting a mantra produces the following benefits:

1. It calms the mind and the emotions
2. It elevates one's consciousness
3. The breath becomes more regular and controlled
4. Mantras are vehicles for expressing our deepest emotions and yearnings
5. Mantras "feed" the higher self and allows it to play a larger role in our daily life.

Advice on Chanting

When you recite a mantra, gently pull in your abdominal muscles, allowing the chest to widen as you vocalize. Breathe through your nose. Exhale evenly while paying attention to your breath. The "melody" of the mantra should be consistent and should not change with each vocalization.

Vocalizing a sacred word in a low, gentle tone increases its power. However, if you find yourself in a place where chanting a mantra is not appropriate (such as in a bus or any other public place) you can recite the sound mentally, and envision it totally enveloping your being as if you were making the sound with your own voice.

Christian Mantras

Ave Maria is considered an expression of love towards the Cosmic Mother, who is often personified by the Virgin Mary. Often used as a blessing for others, it is a powerful mantra that can be vocalized either aloud or silently.

> *Holy Mary, Mother of God*

Nonsectarian English Mantras

> *Oh God Beautiful*
> *Peace*
> *One*
> *I Am*

Arabic Mantras

> *la illaha illa'llah* (There is no God but Allah)
> *Allah Akbar* (There is no one greater than Allah)
> *Allah*

Hebrew Mantras

> *Elohim* (Great Living One)
> *Kodosh* (Holy One)
> *Adonoi* (Lord)
> *Ahavah* (Love)

Shalom (Peace)
Ribbono shel Olem (Master of the Universe or
Source and Substance of All Reality)

Hindu and Buddhist Mantras

OM is a most sacred mantra, and means "the divine energy". It represents the trinity of the physical, mental and spiritual aspects of our being, as well as an individual, universal and transcendental consciousness.

The "O" and the "M" should be sounded for 15 seconds each, making a total of 30 seconds (be sure to inhale deeply before beginning the mantra!).

H. Saraydarian suggests that we vocalize Om three times before beginning meditation and after we complete meditation. He recommends that the first Om be vocalized softly, the second Om louder, and the third still louder. After the three Oms are sounded solemnly, we should visualize their effects during a period of silence. Om can also be sounded silently. If you have heard others recite this mantra (especially a guru or yoga teacher), recall how it sounds and reproduce the sound in your mind.

Hari Om is considered the mantra for healing that will preserve the body and mind in a state of health so that we can attain spiritual realization. In Hindu mythology, *Hari* is the name for the god Vishnu, "the preserver" of the spirit. Chanting "hari" is also viewed as a sign of repentance for our disharmonious actions and attitudes. This mantra can be chanted once per breath, or two sequences per breath to strengthen concentration.

Om Shanti combines the sacred "Om" with the

Sanskrit word for "peace", not unlike the Hebrew word *Shalom*. The words can also be reversed, recited as "Shanti Om."

Om Mani Padmi Hum means "The Jewel of the Lotus," and symbolizes completion and integration. A very powerful mantra, it can should be recited slowly, but in one complete breath.

Om Nama Sivaya is believed to help destroy ignorance. It asks God to help us transform our negative qualities and destroy the obstacles to living a spiritual life. Like the previous mantra, it should be vocalized slowly in one breath.

Om Krishna Guru is recommended when you are seeing a spiritual teacher, either on the concrete level, or as a spirit guide. In addition to "Om", meaning the Supreme Energy, "Krishna" is said to represent the supreme energy manifested in a form becomes personal to us. "Guru" is the Sanskrit term for spiritual teacher.

Om Ah Hung is a mantra used primarily by Tibetan Buddhists. In Buddhism, "Ah" is the source of all speech and sound; it is also a sound of purification, warmth and healing. It represents the energy of expansion and empowerment. "Hung" (pronounced *hoong* with a soft h) is a sound of infinity, enlightenment, and oneness. When Om, Ah and Hung are recited together, the Tibetan monk Tulku Thondup suggests that the length of each sacred word may be varied.

Om Sri Rama Jaya Rama is an appeal to the soul to live according to Divine Will. In the Hindu religion, the god Rama represents the King or Pillar. As a "call to victory" of the Higher Self, this mantra is ideal for a person seeking transformation and self-realization.

Another related mantra would be *Hare Rama*.

AUM is closely related to Om. Swami Sivananda taught that the cosmic AUM is traditionally chanted in three parts, with equal time devoted to each part. When you chant this sacred sound, visualize the *Ah* being chanted in the area of your body near the navel; the *oo*, just above the diaphragm, and the *mm* at the base of the throat. Like the OM, this mantra should be done slowly and clearly in one long complete breath.

Aum nama bhagavate gajananaya namah is a mantra to invoke the presence of the god Ganesha, whose power is believed to remove obstacles and to provide clarity and wisdom when we need to make an important decision in life.

Radha Govinda is a mantra used to discover the Divine within. It is to be chanted with intense feelings of love and devotion, as if the mantra is the key that will open a buried treasure. In Hindu mythology, Radha was the lover of Lord Krishna, and is seen as a symbol of unceasing love for God.

Judeo Christian Mantras

Shalom is one of the most important and beautiful words in the Hebrew language. When used as a mantra, you can elongate the syllables so it is expressed as:

shhhhaaa
looooo
mmmmm

not unlike the OM described above. The syllables can be pronounced in equal lengths, or in varying lengths. The mantra can be chanted in one long breath if desired.

Your Basic Mantra Meditation Technique

As with any other form of mediation, take a few moments to relax. You can use one of the Basic Relaxation Exercises described earlier, or can select another of your choice.

While sitting or standing in a comfortable position, choose a mantra that has significance to you. Recite it aloud clearly and with awareness with your outgoing breath.

Remember that different mantras may require a specific form of expression, so refer to the guidelines for specific mantras offered above. Allow the sound to permeate both the surrounding atmosphere and vibrate deep within your body and mind, so that you feel the power of the manta completely envelop your being.

Continue to recite your mantra for several minutes at first; with practice, you may want to extend your chanting for a half hour or more.

When you wish to stop chanting, make your final recitation and devote several minutes to quiet, rhythmic breathing. You may want to say a short prayer before you conclude your meditation.

Intoning the Name of the Buddha: Namo Amitabha

The repeated intoning of the name of the Buddha is a powerful method of focusing the mind and calming the emotions. The phrase *Namo Amitabha* , means "taking refuge in the boundless life and enlightenment."

The following mantra meditation was inspired by the technique taught by the Won school of Buddhism in Korea. It is intended to help us to discover the Amitabha of our own minds and returning to the paradise of our own original nature.

1. Sit on a chair or on a comfortable cushion placed on the floor. Maintain your posture upright and relax your body and mind. Do not swing of shake your body. You may wish to do one of the Basic Relaxation Exercise, or another form of relaxation before you begin chanting. You may also want to use sacred beads for counting each chant as you recite it.

2. Speaking in your normal voice, concentrate your mind, body, and spirit on intoning the name of the Buddha, linking your entire being with the phrase of *Namo Amitabha*. Recite the phrase slowly and clearly with each outward breath. Merely verbally intoning *Namo Amitabha* without concentration of thought is said to be of little effect, yet the silent repetition of the name of the Buddha can be very powerful if you do so consciously.

3. Allow your mind to completely relax as you chant. Do not imagine the figure of the Buddha as a way of seeking the Buddha from outside, but allow the words to surround you totally, bringing life to your own innate Buddha nature.

4. Continue this chanting meditation for five minutes at first. With practice, you can extend your meditation to ten minutes or longer.

5. When you are finished, take several deep breaths and slowly rise from your seated position.

Teachers of Won Buddhism suggest that you can

intone the name of the Buddha whenever you are annoyed by "delusive thoughts" involving emotions like greed, envy or fear, or while you are walking, standing, sitting or reclining; however you should not chant the Buddha's name if it will distract you from what you are doing, such as driving a car or operating machinery.

Meditation with Sound

One of the most enjoyable methods of practicing mantra meditation is with the aid of audio. Many spiritual organizations and spiritual teachers produce such media.

After doing the Basic Relaxation exercises or another form of relaxation, sit comfortably and turn on the audio, using earphones, earplugs or speakers. Recite the mantra along with the voice(s) on the audio, remaining aware of your breathing and any areas of tension in your body or mind. As you recite the mantra, feel these tensions dissolve.

This meditation can be very inspiring. Allow yourself to fully participate in your experience, yet maintain awareness and your sense of being grounded.

In some cases, you may be inspired to move your body to the words and music; you may even want to express these movements in a form of sacred dance. If, however, you wish to dance, make sure there is plenty of room, so that you do not knock anything over!

Some people can completely lose themselves in a trance-dance, either through the rhythm and repetition of the words that go through their mind; their body keeps moving, but they fall into a meditative state. However, it is important to strive to retain awareness during this and all other types of meditative practice.

Mantra as Prayer

Some mantras may be in the form of many words organized to produce a special effect, not unlike a prayer. One such mantra is recited during group meditation by members of the Meditation Group for the New Age (now Meditation Mount) in Ojai, California:

> One Source, One Power
> Thou in Whom we live and move and have our being,
> The Power Whom can make all things new,
> Give of thine abundance:
> of vision and insight
> of wisdom and joy
> of health and vitality
> of efficient co-workers
> of all the resources necessary
> in order that the Work may be
> adequate to the growing needs
> and the great opportunities of
> the present time
> With faith, we give thanks.

The Great Invocation

The Great Invocation is a powerful mantra that can be an important aspect of any meditation or prayer service. Invoking the forces of Light, Love and Power, the manta not only strengthens these qualities in the world, but within our own beings as well.

Before actually reciting this mantra, take some time to study the meaning of each line. As we develop a greater understanding and appreciation of its power, it will have more power when we recite it.

Recite each line of this mantra carefully and in one breath. As you speak, strive to visualize the image that each line creates in your heart and mind.

From the point of Light within the Mind of God
Let light stream forth into the minds of men.
Let Light descend on Earth.

From the point of Love within the Heart of God
Let love stream forth into the hearts of men.
May Christ return to Earth.

From the center where the Will of God is known
Let purpose guide the little wills of men;
The purpose which the Masters know and serve.

From the center which we call the race of men
Let the Plan of Love and Light work out
And may it seal the door where evil dwells.

Let Light and Love and Power restore the Plan on Earth.

The Navkar Mantra

The Navkar Mantra is the most fundamental mantra in the Jain religion. While reciting the Navkar Mantra, the aspirant bows with respect to Arihantas (destroyers of enemies), Siddhas (liberated souls), Acharyas (spiritual leaders), Upadhyas (monks who have gained a special knowledge of Jain scriptures), Sadhus (male monks) and Sadhvis (female nuns).

The mantra enables us to worship the virtues of all the supreme spiritual people instead of just worshipping one particular person. At the time of recitation, one remembers their virtues and tries to emulate them. This mantra can be recited at any time of the day.

Namo Arihantanam
Namo Siddhanam
Namo Ayriyanam
Namo Uvajjhayanam
Namo Loe Savva Äsahunam
Eso Panch Namokaro
Savva Äpavappanasano
Manglananch Savvesim
Padhamam Havei Mangalam

Translation:

I bow down to Arihanta,
I bow down to Siddha,
I bow down to Acharya,
I bow down to Upadhyaya,
I bow down to Sadhu and Sadhvi.
These five bowing downs,

Destroy all the sins,
Amongst all that is auspicious,
This Navkar Mantra is the foremost.

The Hare Krishna Maha Mantra

One of the world's oldest Hindu scriptures, the *Kalisantarana Upanishad*, teaches that chanting the sixteen words of the hare krishna maha mantra is the prescribed means to counter the evil effects of the time we are presently in.

Popularized in the West by A.C. Bhaktivedanta Swami Prabhupada, leader of the International Society for Krishna Consciousness (ISKCON), the mantra is based the following words that were attributed to Lord Krishna:

Abandon all varieties of religion and just surrender unto Me. I shall deliver you from all sinful reaction. Do not fear.

The mantra reads as follows:

hare krshna hare krshna, krshna krshna,
hare hare,
hare rama hare rama, rama rama, hare
hare,
iti sodasakam namnam,
kali-kalmasa-nasanan,
natah parataropayah, sarva-vedesu drsyate.

The Gāyatrī Mantra

The Gāyatrī is a Vedic hymn that inspires righteous wisdom. Its Sanskrit pronunciation is as follows:

Om Bhoor
Om Bhuvaha
Om Swaha
Tat Savitur Vareniyam Hargo
Devasya Dheemahi Dhiyo Yonaha Prachodayat

Translation:

Almighty God, The giver of life, the remover of
pain and sorrow, the embodiment of
happiness;
O Creator of the Universe, may we receive thy
supreme, sin-destroying light;
May Thou guide my intellect in the right
direction.

A Simple Christian Meditation

This meditation is designed to help make direct contact with one's deepest religious beliefs in a safe, quiet setting.

1. Perform one of the Basic Relaxation exercises or another relaxing technique of your choice.

2. Recite The Lord's Prayer or another prayer of your choice that has a special meaning to you:

Our Father, who art in heaven, hallowed be

69

thy name; thy kingdom come; Thy will be
done on earth as it is in heaven. Give us this
day our daily bread; and forgive us our
trespasses as we forgive those who trespass
against us; and lead us not into temptation,
but deliver us from evil. Amen.

3. As you breathe, visualize the presence of God
both within you and all around you.

4. Next, focus your mind and heart on a specific
word or name that you relate to strongly, such as
Christ, love, Mary or *holy.* Repeat this word like a
mantra as you breathe, using one repetition per
outward breath. Feel the essence of this word or name
permeate your entire being.

5. After several minutes, conclude your meditate

6. on. Express your gratitude at this time, if you
wish.

The Centering Prayer Meditation

This meditation is based on the spiritual practice of an
early Christian monk. Mystics have described this
exercise as "leading us to the heart of God."

The major purpose of this meditation is to express
our innate desire to know what we call God, the Great
Spirit or Absolute Truth.

1. Begin this meditation by sitting on the floor or
in a comfortable chair with your eyes closed, being
aware of your breathing. Work with your breath for

several minutes as you slowly relax.

2. Imagine that you are sitting in the sky, above a cloud. This is the "cloud of forgetting," to which you will send all of your body tensions, the worries of the day. Continue to do this, until you feel totally relaxed. Continue breathing with awareness.

3. Now imagine another cloud above you, which is the "cloud of unknowing." In your mind's eye, imagine this cloud interpenetrating your entire being, including your body, thoughts, feelings and spirit.

4. Remind yourself that you are seeking for the truth and that you knowledge is limited at this time. Allow yourself to connect with the place within that is yearning to know the truth or the answer to a question that has eluded you up to now.

5. Allow this feeling to blend with your desire to connect with the Great Spirit or God, where you will find the answer to your question.

6. Gently vocalize a word or short phrase that has religious significance for you. It may be a mantra, the name of a saint, or a phrase as simple as "God," "love," or "shalom." Repeat this word or phrase gently, but with deep feeling, as if it were the key to open the door to Truth.

7. Allow your yearning to penetrate the "cloud of unknowing" that lies between yourself and the Great Spirit. Continue paying attention to your breathing, as you repeat your prayer or mantra.

8. Whenever something comes to mind, whether a childhood hurt, or a thought or feeling that causes disharmony, repeat your mantra or prayer and direct it into the cloud of forgetting.

9. Be aware of the possibility of receiving love and wisdom from the Great Spirit as you continue this

prayerful meditation. Allow it to permeate your being as you breathe.

  10.   When you intuitively feel that the time is right, slowly conclude your meditation with an expression of thanks.

When practiced regularly, this meditation can help you to connect to the essence of Spirit and helps you to integrate it into your daily life.

Listening to the Divine

Few of us realize that spiritual help is, as a teacher once said, "no more than your next breath away." The following simple meditation is designed to help us come into contact with Divine energy, whether or not we believe in a Universal God, or the "God within."

  1. Practice one of the Basic Relaxation exercises or another relaxation exercise of your choice.

  2. Recite a short prayer of your choice which you feel brings you into closer contact with the Divine. You may choose something like The Lord's Prayer, or a simple prayer like "I ask to be open to the presence of God in my life at this time."

  3. As you watch your breathing, verbally express a word (or words) that reflect a specific spiritual quality or attribute that you want to more fully manifest in your life right now. Repeat this word or phrase out loud (and with feeling) several times until you feel that it has become more integrated into your consciousness.

4. Now, in silence, contemplate the meaning and deeper ramifications of your chosen word or phrase. What does it mean to you? How can it manifest in your life? How will it change you in the future? If you find your mind wandering from the subject, repeat the word or phrase aloud again.

5. After several minutes, allow yourself to conclude your meditation. End your meditation session with a prayer of thanks, or one that encompasses your chosen word, such as "I pray that love can more fully permeate my life," or "I pray to be more aware of opportunities to be generous today."

Forgiveness Meditations

Forgiveness has always been considered one of the most spiritual acts of life, in part because it is often not easy to do. When we are injured by another person, many of us hold a grudge for days, weeks, months or even a lifetime. When this happens, we harden our hearts, which can make us lose contact with our innate loving and Divine nature.

Meditation for Forgiving Another

The following meditation is designed to help facilitate forgiveness. Until you have gained considerable experience in both meditation and your chosen spiritual practice, the person you wish to forgive should not be someone who has committed a major wrong against you, but rather a person with whom you have had a minor conflict like an argument or disagreement. As you practice this meditation regularly, you can deal with those whom have hurt you more deeply.

1. Sit comfortably. If you are sitting on a mat, cross your legs; if you are sitting on a comfortable hard-backed chair, place your feet flat on the floor. Your spine should be straight, your shoulders relaxed, and your eyes should be positioned straight ahead. Fold your hands lightly in your lap or place them, palms up, on your thighs.

2. Gently close your eyes. Be aware of your breathing, which should be from the diaphragm. Don't try to control your breathing, but be aware of its rhythm. Maintain awareness on your breath for a few moments.

3. Now, slowly "scan" your body, moving downwards from the top of your head.

Be aware of your feet for a few moments, and then slowly extend it downwards to your neck, your chest, your shoulders, your arms, your hands; your abdomen, your lower back, your pelvic area; your thighs, your legs, and your feet. Wherever you feel tension, "breathe" into that area, visualizing relaxation and warmth reaching that part of your body. This process should take several minutes.

3. When your body is fully relaxed and aware of itself, bring your attention back to your breath for a few moments.

4. Now bring to mind someone who has wronged you recently, and whom you have not yet forgiven.

5. Review the unpleasant exchange or situation as it occurred, without exaggerating or otherwise altering any element.

6. Gently ask yourself the following questions:

"How might this exchange have occurred in a more positive way?"

"What could I have said (or not said) or done (or not done) to have produced a different result?"

"How might I have contributed to the problem due to feelings of pride, fear or self-will?"

"How might the other person have responded to any positive gestures on my part?"

7. At this point, take a few deep breaths, and say aloud: "I wish to forgive, as I wish to be forgiven."

8. Allow yourself to feel compassion and forgiveness for the person, even if it is just a small amount of forgiveness at first (this meditation can be repeated whenever you wish).

9. Then take a few more deep breaths, slowly open your eyes, and return to everyday reality once more.

If you can, communicate with that person and offer your forgiveness. As a result of the meditation, you may also want to ask for forgiveness yourself, since you may have discovered that you contributed to the unpleasant situation.

If the other person refuses to communicate with you, try again another time. If the other person insists on holding a grudge against you, know that you have done your best and get on with your life.

If the other person is no longer living, forgive him or her "in the spirit." You may wish to express your forgiveness in a more concrete way by visiting the person's gravesite or by donating money to a charity in his or her memory.

Self-forgiveness Meditation

While forgiving other people is not always easy, forgiving oneself is often more difficult. The following meditation is designed to help us cultivate self-forgiveness and begin to free ourselves of the limits that an unforgiving attitude imposes on our life.

1. Sit comfortably in a straight-backed chair or on a meditation mat. Perform one of the Basic Relaxation exercises presented earlier in this book. Be aware of your breathing, and take deep yet gentle breaths.

2. As you continue to watch your breathing, allow yourself to consider one aspect in your life that you truly regret: it may be something you did to another person, a limiting or negative attitude, or a sin of omission that you regret deeply.

3. Allow this memory to surface, without judging it in any way. Be aware of your emotional and physical reactions as you continue to watch your breathing. Examine the issues behind the regret and see it as part of your life history.

4. Then ponder on how you can atone for this source of regret. Does it involve asking forgiveness from another person? Does it involve a change of attitude or belief? Does it involve an act of redemption?

Also, ask yourself if you may be overreacting to the original situation. Are you carrying a burden of guilt for too long? Might there be a different perspective that will allow you to move forward in your life? Allow your thoughts and feelings to come up, and record them in a journal.

5. Ask for help in transcending this regret into a

stepping stone to help you reach a new level of being. Say a prayer like "I pray to forgive myself."

6. As you conclude your meditation, take a few deep breaths and stretches before you get up again.

Goodness Meditation

Many of us underestimate our gifts and do not acknowledge our good deeds and other accomplishments. While not intended as an "ego trip", the following meditation is designed to help us to "take stock" of the good things we have done in our life.

1. Perform one of the Basic Relaxation exercises described earlier. As you watch your breathing, pray "I ask to acknowledge the good I have done in my life."

2. With pen in hand, begin to write down all the beautiful, loving things you have done in your life. These may include acts of compassion and generosity, right attitudes, or acts of courage: anything that you feel particularly good about (even if you might have forgotten it). Be aware of any period in your life that was especially rich in good deeds and loving actions.

3. After several minutes of "brainstorming" read the list back to yourself. Say to yourself, "I acknowledge the goodness within me." At this point, you may wish to express gratitude for your life, and your innate gift of goodness. Ask the Great Spirit for more opportunities to express goodness in your life.

Meditations of Gratitude

Many of us experience feelings of melancholy from time to time. We sometimes focus on our failings and highlight what is missing from our lives rather than acknowledging the positive aspects of ourselves and what is good in our life. While not seeking to escape from our problems, the following meditations are designed to help us come into contact with the many positive aspects of our life as it is at the present time and to feel gratitude for what we have.

I.

1. Do one of the Basic Relaxation exercises described earlier.

2. Say a simple prayer like "I pray to be aware of what I am grateful for in my life."

3. Pen and journal in hand, begin writing a list of what you have to be grateful for. This list can include aspects of your personality you are happy with, the presence of certain people in your life, your pet, certain possessions you have, your job, knowledge or insights you may have gained, your health, the favorite tree in your front yard, and whatever else may come into your mind.

4. Do not limit the flow of ideas, simply allowing your active mind to "brainstorm" as you record your impressions in your journal. Allow several minutes for this exercise. When you are finished, read over each impression either silently or out loud.

5. When you have finished reading your list, devote a minute or so to quiet breathing. Conclude your meditation with a pray of thanks.

II.

1. Perform one of the Basic Relaxation exercises described earlier.

2. On a piece of paper, write down the names of every person who has been kind to you, either today or during your lifetime. These include people who may have done special favors for you, listened to your troubles, helped you with a problem, gave you a hug when you needed it or who have performed an especially caring act that you have never been able to forget.

3. When you have finished, you may read their name(s), either singly or as a group, and say "May (he/she/they/name) receive God's grace," "I Thank God for having (him/her/them/name) in my life" or another expression of your own choosing.

Angel Meditations

Whenever we go to sleep, our soul enters the subtle realms of existence where angelic forces reside. Angels have been an important aspect of religious belief since ancient times. They have long been considered "God's messengers" who offer us protection, guidance and healing.

The following meditations, done as we are about to go to sleep at night, are designed to help us make contact with the angelic realms and open ourselves to their blessing during sleep.

I.

1. While lying in bed, close your eyes and breathe deeply for several minutes. Visualize areas of tension in your body and allow them to relax one by one.

2. When you feel relaxed and in a receptive mood, recite a favorite prayer of your choice or chant a mantra that is especially meaningful to you. You can also pray: "Oh, Powers of Love, I pray to commune with the Angels tonight." Continue your breathing with this feeling in your heart.

3. In your mind's eye, visualize an angelic being. It may be the type of angel you have seen in religious art, or the angel may take another form, such as a core of pure, white light. Imagine yourself communing with this angel, allowing the angel's energy to permeate your entire being. Feel the healing, the lightness and the comfort that is enveloping you at this time. Continue to breathe and relax.

4. At this point, many people fall asleep. However, if you are still awake, allow your consciousness to bring up a problem that you have been having, or an issue that you have been having difficulty with, such as a health problem, a difficult decision that has been on your mind, or a concern you have for a friend or relative. Visualize the problem being offered to the angelic light. At this point, you can say "I pray for assistance in resolving this problem in the light of God's will" or simply "I pray for healing and wholeness."

5. Continue to breathe comfortable, deep breaths, and allow yourself to drift off to sleep.

II.

1. While you are lying in bed, close your eyes and breathe deeply for several minutes. Visualize areas of tension in your body and allow them to relax one by one.

2. Review the day's events in your mind. If anyone has wronged you in any way during the day, send them feelings of compassion and forgiveness. If you have wronged others, feel remorse for your actions, being careful not to wallow in guilt. Affirm that you do not want to repeat this action and pray to be more aware so you do not repeat it in the future. If you have hurt another person by your action, resolve to ask forgiveness of that person. Continue to breathe deeply.

3. Now visualize four angels above you, watching over you as you sleep. They represent four Divine qualities that are with us always.

On your right, feel the presence of the Archangel Michael, representing Divine Mercy, which forgives your mistakes.

On your left, feel the presence of the Archangel Gabriel, representing Divine Strength, protecting you from worry and fear.

Behind you, feel the fiery presence of the angel Uriel, representing Divine Light, illuminating your soul with wisdom and insight.

In front of you, feel the presence of the Archangel Raphael, the angel of Healing, who promotes integration and wholeness, as well as physical, emotional and spiritual renewal.

Besides all four angels, strive to be conscious of the presence of God, Who both includes and transcends these four Divine Aspects. At this point, you may wish to say a statement like "God is One," "There is One God," "Thank You, Great Spirit, and Your Holy Angels, for Your blessings as I sleep."

Repeat this meditation until you fall asleep.

When you awaken in the morning, you will often feel alive and refreshed. You may also experience a feeling of resolution (or the beginnings of resolution) regarding any problems you may have been dealing with.

This feeling can be easily brought into your morning meditation as you continue a benign cycle of healing and blessing from the angelic realms.

Guardian Angel Meditations

Some Western religions teach of the existence of guardian angels: one or more personal angels who guide us and protect us throughout our life. In Exodus (23:20) Yahweh declares to Moses: "Behold, I send an Angel before thee, to keep thee in the way, and to bring thee into the place which I have prepared. Beware of him and obey his voice..."

Guardian angels have long been recognized as guides who help oversee the processes of our personal evolution, and offer us guidance, support and comfort as we tread the often difficult path of living in the day to day world. The following meditations are designed to enable us to commune with our Guardian angel.

Invisible Helper Meditation

We mentioned earlier that whenever we go to sleep, our soul enters the subtle realms of existence where we can commune with angels or God's "messengers."

The Theosophical teacher C.W. Leadbeater taught that many of us can work with angels when we are asleep and help them assist humans and other living forms that are in need. He believed that during natural disasters like floods or earthquakes, humans can assist angels in offering comfort, protection and even practical guidance by working with them on a soul level to help relieve their suffering.

This assistance may not only be used during natural disasters. As a spiritual law teaches that like often attracts like, we may be asked to serve compatible individuals literally anywhere in the world with any type of problem.

The following meditation, done as we are about to go to sleep, is designed to help us make contact with the angelic realms and serve as "invisible helpers" while we are asleep.

1. While you are lying in bed, close your eyes and breathe deeply for several minutes. Recite a favorite prayer of your choice or chant a mantra that is especially meaningful to you. At this point you can simply ask, "Oh, Powers of Love, I pray to serve as an Invisible Helper tonight if it is God's Will."

2. At this point, you may feel compassion for those who were involved in a natural disaster or other mass tragedy. Or you may feel the pain of a friend or relative who is experiencing suffering or grief. Feel the love and compassion welling up in your heart and visually

send them your love and support. You may repeat either vocally or to yourself, "I pray to be of service to those who are suffering."

3. Continue to breathe comfortable, deep breaths, and allow yourself to drift off to sleep.

Some people who ask to serve as invisible helpers may experience vivid dreams that reveal their experience during the hours of sleep. If you have such an experience, write it down or record it digitally.

Others simply awaken feeling as though they accomplished something important during the night, although they may not have any recollection of what actually occurred. If you are one of these people, don't worry about it. It is not really important that you remember a good deed. The point is that you have offered to help alleviate suffering in the world and left the rest to the angels!

Meditation to Protect a Loved One

1.   Perform Step 1 of the previous meditation. Say a prayer such as "I pray for Divine protection for [name] today."

2.   Envision the white light in the room.

3.   Visualize an image of loved one being surrounded by this globe of shimmering white light. If your loved one is flying in an airplane, for example, and you are concerned about his or her safety, visualize the light surrounding both the person and the aircraft. Know that your loved one is in God's hands and is completely safe. Continue this visualization for several minutes or until you feel comfortable about your loved one's welfare. If you wish to recite a prayer asking for protection, do so at

this time.

4. As you conclude the meditation, you may wish to say a brief prayer of thanks. Take several deep breaths and stretch for a moment before rising.

Eating Meditation

As many gourmets can attest, eating can be a spiritual experience. Yet for most of us, we eat mostly to survive, and are often unaware of our food when we eat it. The following meditation is designed to help us feel a deeper connection with the food that nourishes and sustains us.

1. Sit quietly with food before you. Ideally, confine your meditation to a single type of natural food at first, like an apple, an olive a carrot or a few nuts in the shell.

2. Observe the food set before you, and take note of the color, texture and aroma. If possible, hold it in your hand and offer thanks to the Great Spirit for the food that you are about to take into your body. Express gratitude to the life form that you are about to eat.

3. In your mind's eye, imagine tracing the origins of the food. If you are about to eat an olive, for example, picture the olive tree rooted deep in the earth. Imagine it in its natural surroundings, including the sun, rains and wind. Imagine the olive being picked at its moment of ripeness, and give thanks to the harvester as well as those who prepare the olive and brought it to you today. Devote several minutes to this exercise.

4. Take a small bite out of the food. Allow your

mouth to experience it fully: the taste, the juice, the texture. Allow your taste buds to enjoy it while appreciating the entirety of your experience. Chew the food slowly and thoroughly. When the time is right, slowly swallow the food, acknowledging that it is becoming part of your body. Feel your connection to the food, and also feel your gratitude for nourishment; at the same time, feel your connectedness with the source of the food, such as the olive tree or apple tree. Continue to experience the food in this manner until it is completely eaten.

5. Give thanks to the Great Spirit and to the life of the food that you have eaten. Pray that its sacrifice will enable you to be or service to others.

6. Throughout this meditation, be aware of your desire to rush this process and be conscious of any feelings that might come up while you are doing this meditation. Do I feel uneasy or guilty about eating? How do I feel when I take another life to sustain my own? How do I disassociate myself from what I eat? Do I eat quietly, or do I "pack it in" before moving on to another activity? How do I abuse my relationship with food?"

With regular practice, this meditation can be expanded to include different foods that are made up of more than one ingredient, such as bread, soup or tea. If practiced regularly, every single meal can evolve to becoming a meditation that will help expand and deepen your awareness towards the life forms that nourish and sustain you. Eating food in a meditative way will improve digestion and increase overall enjoyment. At the same time, you will eat only what you really need rather than consume excessive amounts.

Meditation for Drivers

During a talk at San Diego State University some years ago, the Indian teacher J. Krishnamurti turned his focus to meditation. With enthusiasm, he extolled the virtues of meditation, and mentioned that one could meditate anywhere: at home, at school, on a bus, and even while driving a car. Upon noticing the surprised reaction of some members of the audience to his reference to driving, he quickly added with a laugh, "but be awfully careful."

With modern distractions like smart phones, texting, internet connectivity and an increasing lack of courtesy on the nation's highways, driving (especially in heavy traffic and on the freeways) has become a challenge for many.

Yet for those who drive, it is important to know that meditation does not imply "spacing out" behind the wheel. Because the goal of meditation is focused awareness, it can actually increase our potential for safety.

In addition to helping make the journey more enjoyable, meditation can help reduce stress and enable us become both more forgiving and more considerate of others when we are behind the wheel. The following meditation is best done while alone.

1. After you settle into your seat, take several deep breaths, noting any areas of tension in your body. Breathe into those areas of tension, allowing your breathing to dissolve the stress.

87

2. Pray, "I ask for protection on my journey today, and I may I be attentive behind the wheel."

3. Keep your radio, cell phone and other electronic devices off as you drive. Be aware of how you are driving, taking special note of speed, anger, impatience and daydreaming. If you catch yourself daydreaming, gently move your attention back to your speed, the road, and the other drivers around you. Try to anticipate their moves. Send good feelings to other drivers, including those who would ordinarily make you angry or frustrated.

Whenever you reach a stop sign or stoplight, take several gentle breaths and review how you are feeling. If you feel tense or anxious, take several deep breaths, and exhale while making a sound like "aahhhh."

4. When you arrive at your destination, take a moment to give thanks for a safe trip. Turn off the ignition and mindfully leave your car.

Airplane Meditations

Meditating on an airplane offers unique opportunities. Flying high above the Earth, you are in a relatively safe environment that is both quiet and comfortable, yet offering a unique perspective of the planet on which we live, including the geography, weather patterns, air currents and the state of the environment over which we pass. Certain views – such as clouds, rivers and mountains- can be very inspiring.

The time you spend on an air journey (especially when traveling alone) can be a form of "suspended animation," where you are disengaged from your daily life responsibilities as well as with the people you normally spend your time with.

Psychically, the stratosphere is a place of rarified energy that facilitates spiritual activities like prayer, meditation and creative visualization. The following meditations are designed to help you take advantage of this special airborne environment and to become aware of new perspectives regarding personal perceptions, problems and aspirations.

I.

Sitting comfortably in your seat, close your eyes and breathe deeply yet quietly. Visualize yourself as you are at the moment, moving high above the earth in total safety, feeling as though you are in the hands of God. Be aware of turbulence or other movements of the aircraft, knowing that you are safe and moving forward on your journey through the vast, unlimited open sky.

See yourself as free from earthly obligations, including your job, your family, your daily responsibilities. You are almost in a state of benign suspension, of emptiness. You are part of life, yet at the same time, detached from it.

II.

Close your eyes and remain aware of your breathing. Allow yourself to bring up a thought, or a problem that concerns you. Strive to view it from your present state of detached awareness.

As you breathe comfortably, ask how you might deal with this problem or concern from this detached perspective. Ask: "Can I view this issue from my unique perspective of detachment at this time?" "What can I say or do to improve the situation?" "How can I move the situation towards a new level of resolution?"

Continue to breathe and open your eyes. You are in the world, yet moving high above the earth. It is truly a special experience. Conclude your meditation and record your impressions in a notebook.

III.

As you breathe evenly, pray to be open to new ideas and new directions. Close your eyes and allow yourself to envision what you would like to see happen in your life. Do you wish to encourage the emergence of a hidden talent or ability? Do you have a project you would like to begin (or finish)? Is there a relationship you wish to pursue (or change the one you are presently involved in)? Is there a career goal towards which you are striving?

As you continue to watch your breathing, allow your mind to quietly explore the issue. How do you relate to it? What is blocking your fulfillment? How can you see it happen? As you play with these thoughts, be open to any new ideas or perspectives that may come into your consciousness. Enjoy the journey and feel gratitude for the opportunity to explore these important issues in your life.

After several minutes, open your eyes and look around the plane. Then record your impressions and insights in a journal.

Meditations for Right Livelihood

Choosing a career is one of the most important decisions a person can make. Ideally, a career should be more than simply earning a living, but also way to learn, to grow, and to utilize our interests, talents and abilities.

The concept of *Right Livelihood* was first introduced by the Buddha thousands of years ago. Since that time, right livelihood has been viewed as a way of life that develops a sense of self-worth, does good for society, and fosters respect for all living beings. According to Danaan Perry and Lila Forest in *The Earthstewards Handbook*, right livelihood needs to encompass the following aspects of our life:

1. produce something of personal benefit rather than just material benefits to others
2. provide a fair return which fulfills one's personal needs while not encouraging personal greed
3. give us a sense of being a valued part of the local and larger community
4. develop a touchstone of deep experience by which to measure other situations in life
5. provide genuine personal satisfaction and self-fulfillment
6. increase skill and the development of one's talents and faculties
7. give expression to the values by which we live

The following meditations are designed to help us develop a deeper sense of right livelihood in our lives.

For those searching for a career path

1. Sit in a comfortable position on a straight-backed chair or meditation cushion. Do one of the Basic Relaxation exercises described earlier in this book, or another of your choice.

2. Begin to ponder on the right career for you. Ask yourself: What are my major interests? What are my strongest talents? What types of activities give me pleasure and fulfillment? What kind(s) of work would I *really* like to do? How can I integrate my spiritual beliefs into a career path? What concrete steps do I need to take in order to move ahead?

3. Allow your ideas and feelings to come to the surface, without judging them or limiting them in any way. Record them in your journal.

4. Continue this meditation exercise for ten minutes. Take a few deep breaths, stretch and slowly leave the seated meditation position.

For those already on a career path

1. Sit in a comfortable position on a straight-backed chair or meditation cushion. Do one of the Basic Relaxation exercises described earlier in this book, or another of your choice.

2. Begin to ponder on your career, writing your observations in a journal. Rather than focusing on changing it, think about what originally drew you to it in the first place. Ask yourself: How does it mobilize my talents? Did I originally feel passion towards you work? What are the sources of dissatisfaction at the present time? Are there ways to deal with these

sources? If so, what are they? How can I make my career more in line with the teaching about right livelihood? Do I need a total change of direction? If so, what do I need to do in order to take the next step?

3. Allow your thoughts and feelings to surface without judging them or limiting them in any way. Some may provide vital information to enable you to take the next step in your career direction.

4. Continue this meditation exercise for ten minutes. Take a few deep breaths, stretch and slowly leave the seated meditation position.

Healing Meditations

Meditation can be a powerful tool for healing, because it allows us to explore the deeper issues of health and disease. As opposed to curing, healing is a *process*, rather than a goal. It encompasses the entire spectrum of the human being, including the physical, emotional, mental and spiritual.

Healing implies viewing our situation in a wider perspective that goes beyond the treatment of symptoms, to embrace all aspects of one's life. Rather than becoming fixated on symptoms (which often can distract us from the healing process), healing means learning from the crisis (or from the symptom) we experience rather than trying to control or eliminate it. It involves developing the flexibility we need to change the attitudes which keep us out of touch with our innate intelligence, respect and love.

Healing also involves accepting pain or discomfort while expanding our perspective to learn what our suffering has to teach us. Rather than trying to compete with symptoms or pain from the outside (through therapeutic means, be they natural or otherwise), healing implies taking responsibility for growth and change from the inside. When viewed in this perspective, meditation can be a powerful tool to facilitate self-healing and inner growth.

Healing with Visualization

Creative visualization is often used in a healing meditation. Louise L. Hay, the author of *You Can Heal Your Life* and other books, outlines the three basic parts of a positive healing visualization, which anyone can adapt to their individual needs:

1. An image of the problem or pain or dis-ease, or the dis-eased part of the body.
2. An image of a positive force eliminating this problem.
3. An image of the body being rebuilt to perfect health, then seeing the body move through life with ease and energy.

Remember that positive visualization can incorporate literal images, symbolic images related to treatment, or abstract images. One universal image you can use it is a source of bright, white healing light, and imagine it shining around (and through) every aspect of your being.

A powerful tool to this type of visualization meditation is "The Divine Light Invocation Mantra," taught by Swami Sivananda Radha:

I am created by Divine Light
I am sustained by Divine Light
I am protected by Divine Light
I am surrounded by Divine Light
I am ever growing into Divine Light.

Some people may wish to visualize being healed by Jesus Christ or the Healing Buddha, while others may want to incorporate saints, yogis, angels or other spiritual beings in their healing meditations.

Accessing Healing Guidance

Many of us are taught to believe that healing has to do with our physician's level of expertise or the complexity of the medication we are given. We often overlook the fact that it is our own body that is doing the healing: healing is essentially *an inside job*. We may call on a health professional to assist us initiate and maintain the healing process, yet it is we ourselves who are doing the healing.

This simple meditation is designed to help us to take greater responsibility for our healing, and can to help us access inner wisdom regarding our health situation.

1. Sit comfortably in a chair or on a meditation mat. Do one of the Basic Relaxation exercises described earlier in this book, or use another relaxation method of your choice.

2. After you feel comfortable and relaxed, say clearly, slowly and purposefully: "I am a self-healing being. I have an unlimited capacity to heal myself. I pray to access my body's innate healing power to the

fullest." You may want to repeat this prayer several times so that it becomes more integrated in your consciousness.

3. Devote several minutes to receptive silence. Chances are that many thoughts and feelings will come, including fear, anger, frustration, doubt, and judgments. You may have feelings of resistance to heal, or even a desire to remain sick. By the same token, you may experience inspiration and lightness, along with a feeling that you are open to new ideas and possibilities; some may involve practical guidance that can facilitate your healing and assist your health practitioner to help you heal. Allow these thoughts and feelings to surface, without judging or limiting them. Write down your impressions in a notebook. Some of these ideas or impressions can eventually be subjects of meditation themselves.

4. When you feel ready to end your meditation, take several deep breaths before slowing getting up.

Repeat this daily meditation as often as you need to. Since self-healing may involve many personal issues like childhood hurts, poor self-image, negative attitudes, wrong assumptions, and anger towards oneself, family or friends, this meditation can serve as a vehicle for self-exploration and self-discovery as we embark on our personal healing journey.

Accessing Deeper Healing Wisdom

This meditation is similar to the previous one, although it is intended to be used by those who have already done some exploration with the previous method.

Many of feel victimized when we are ill or have suffered an accident, and are eager to have unpleasant symptoms relieved as soon as possible. Yet we can also use our pain and suffering as a springboard to learn more about ourselves and to develop new goals and areas of interest. This meditation allows us to move deeper into the healing process, and to work with specific issues that may have come to our attention.

1. Sit comfortably in a chair or on a meditation mat. Do one of the Basic Relaxation exercises described earlier in this book, or use another relaxation method of your choice.

2. After you feel comfortable and relaxed, say clearly, slowly and purposefully: "I pray to discover the inner meanings of my health problem." You may want to repeat this prayer several times so that it becomes more integrated into your consciousness.

3. As you breathe quietly and evenly, allow yourself to ponder your prayer request. Rather than feel victimized by your health problem, ask if there might be a pattern or rhythm to your symptoms, especially if you have suffered a similar health problem previously. Is your health problem offering you any opportunities for personal growth? Are there any positive components to your health problem, such as time off from work, greater self-nurturing, or changes in your thinking and goals? What new insights have you gained about your life and relationships? What would you like to change about your life if you could? Are there any areas of interest you would like to pursue? Allow your responses to surface, without judging or limiting them. Write down your impressions in a notebook.

4. When you feel ready to end your meditation, take several deep breaths before slowing getting up.

As with the previous exercise, repeat this daily meditation as often as you need to.

Healing Light Meditation

This powerful meditation is designed to enable you to access the powers of healing in the universe.

1. Sit comfortably either in a straight backed chair or on a cushion or mat. Once in a comfortable posture, do one of the Basic Relaxation exercises described earlier.
2. As you sit quietly, visualize a tiny point of pure, white light located about six inches (15 cm) above your head.
3. Visualize this light as getting brighter. As it brightens, it sends out strong beams of light just in front of you, to your right, to your left and behind you. You see yourself surrounded by brilliant white light on all sides of you. It makes you feel both secure and blessed.
4. As you continue to be aware of your breathing, inhale this light through your nose. Feel the light entering your lungs and penetrating every part of your body. Feel its healing power. Feel its wisdom.
5. Now, visualize a blue light beginning to move through your body, exiting through the soles of your feet. This is a cleansing light, and contains any negative thoughts, inner disharmony, pain and tension that you may have been holding in. Breathe in the white light, and exhale the blue light, knowing that

you are being healed by the incoming "white" breath and cleansed by the outgoing "blue" breath.

6. Continue this exercise for several minutes. As you slowly come out of your meditation, visualize the light fading until it becomes the tiny point of light above your head. Express gratitude to the light, and ask that it remain with you throughout the day. Know, too, that you can access its power through this meditation exercise at any time.

Healing Hand Meditation

The following meditation is similar to the previous one, except that it involves the use of your own hand for channeling additional healing energy to a specific area of your body that is ill or is in pain.

1. Sit comfortably either in a straight backed chair or on a cushion or mat. Once in a comfortable posture, do one of the Basic Relaxation exercises described earlier.

2. As you sit quietly, visualize a tiny point of pure, white light located about six inches (15 cm) above your head.

3. Visualize this light as getting brighter. As it brightens, it sends out strong beams of light just in front of you, to your right, to your left and behind you. You see yourself surrounded by brilliant white light on all sides of you. It makes you feel both secure and blessed.

4. As you continue to be aware of your breathing, inhale this light through your nose. Feel the light entering your lungs and penetrating every part of your body. Feel its healing power. Feel its wisdom.

5. Imagine that your right hand is receiving an extra abundance of healing energy; it is almost as though the healing light is radiating out of your hand.

6. Gently place your hand on an area of your body or mind that needs healing, and envision this light as penetrating that area, bathing it with and healing. If you have been feeling pain in that area, imagine it to be dissipated by the energy from your hand. Remember that the light may make you feel either warm or cool.

7. Continue this exercise for several minutes. As you slowly come out of your meditation, visualize the light fading until it becomes the tiny point of light above your head.

Meditation for Managing Pain

1. Sit comfortably either in a straight backed chair or on a cushion or mat. Once in a comfortable posture, do one of the Basic Relaxation exercises described earlier.

2. Remember an event or experience that you thoroughly enjoyed. It may be a time that made you happy, a special meal, or an experience with a special person you remember with fondness. Recall the details of that experience, including sights, sounds, colors and tastes. Recall the feelings that you had, and savor the memories.

3. Now, move your visualization to another event, such as a celebration. Recall the laughter, the play, the feelings of happiness you had. Savor your memory of the experience, and bring it into the present moment.

4. Visualize some of your accomplishments in life, or aspects of your life that are special sources of pride

and happiness for you. Allow yourself to feel good about yourself and your accomplishments.

5. Continue to be aware of your breathing. Visualize these good feelings flow into the area of your body that is in pain. Feel their warmth and their healing power. Know that these memories and experiences are parts of your total being; they make up your living history.

6. Slowly conclude your meditation. Take several deep breaths, stretch, and slowly rise from your meditation posture.

Inner Wisdom Healing Meditation

This meditation helps us to come into contact with our body's inner wisdom; the ultimate source of healing.

1. Sit comfortably either in a straight backed chair or on a cushion or mat. Once in a comfortable posture, do one of the Basic Relaxation exercises described elsewhere in this book.

2. As you take full, deep and easy breaths, feel your body relaxing totally. At the same time, feel the aliveness of your body: your energy is flowing, your emotions are stable, your mind is alert.

3. Perform a "mental scan" of your body. Be aware of the myriad activities of circulation, digestion, elimination, temperature regulation, and protection that your brain, nervous system, immune system, muscles and organs are doing on their own, without you even having to think about it. Feel your body's ability to maintain and heal itself.

4. Allow yourself to experience a sense of gratitude and wonder. Tell your body that you are grateful.

5. Now, ask your body *what it needs* at this time to facilitate healing. You may need to ask more than once. Be open to receiving any answer that may come up; they may involve proper nutrition, rest, exercise, therapeutic procedures, or herbs. Write your impressions in a notebook.

Meditation for Dealing with Trauma and Shock

Life involves constant change. Yet major changes, such as sudden trauma, unexpected loss or surprising news can be difficult to deal with.

When faced with sudden or traumatic change, find a quiet place and perform one or more of the Basic Relaxation exercises described earlier. At the same time, strive to focus your attention on the present moment, being especially aware of your thoughts and feelings at this time. Allow them to surface and record them in your journal.

After several minutes (or for as long as this process lasts) offer these feelings to god or the Great Spirit. Ask for assistance in helping you to deal with your situation (you may wish to express simply "Lord, please help me!") Continue your breathing for several minutes before concluding your meditation.

Repeat as necessary.

Swami Yogananda Healing Meditation

This healing meditation technique is based on one introduced by Paramahansa Yogananda, the respected Indian teacher and author of the acclaimed book *Autobiography of a Yogi*. It is primarily intended to enable you to help heal another.

1. Sit upright in a comfortable, straight-backed chair.

2. Focus your attention on the "spiritual eye," which is the area between your eyebrows. It is also the "will power" center of the body.

3. After several minutes, think of the spiritual eye of the person you wish to send healing energy to (often holding a photograph of this person in front of you will help you to better visualize them).

4. Don't think of the person's disease, but think instead of the healing process that is trying to strengthen the innate healing power of the person.

5. Visualize healing light moving through your medulla oblongata at the base of your brain; then draw that healing light through the point between your two eyebrows. Send the healing light through this center into the spiritual eye of the person you wish to help.

6. Devote several minutes to filling their whole body with healing light.

7. Recite the following affirmation:

> O Infinite Spirit
> Thou art omnipotent
> Thou art in all thy children.
> Thou art in (name of the person to be healed)
> Manifest Thy heavenly presence in his/her
> body, mind and soul.

8. Then rub your hands together briskly until you feel a magnetic charge in your hands; this will probably manifest as a warm, tingling sensation. Hold your hands up, palms out, to send the healing energy

103

to the recipient.

9. Chant AUM three times.

10. As you continue to hold up your hands, move them up and down in space.

11. Visualize sending the energy as long as you feel inspired to do so.

Group Healing Meditations

The Theosophical Order of Service (TOS) is made up of members of the Theosophical Society, an international organization formed to serve as a nucleus for the universal brotherhood of humanity, to encourage the study of comparative religion, philosophy and science and to investigate the unexplained laws of nature and powers latent in humanity.

Because the Theosophical Society is non-political and does not involve itself in politics or social action, the TOS, as a separate organization, serves as a vehicle to encourage active service in areas like ecology, human rights, animal welfare and healing.

The following two group rituals, with minor variations, are used by members of the TOS to invoke the powers of healing angels or *devas*, which mean "shining ones" in Sanskrit.

These meditation rituals, which are Christian in tone, are very powerful. The first of the two can be easily adapted for individual use.

Ritual for Invoking the Healing Angels

Preparation

A white or gold box is to be placed in the center of the table. The names of persons to be healed are placed inside the box. A gold chalice is placed on top of the box, and a white cloth is placed over both the chalice and the box. Traditionally, a white candle is placed on either side of the box. Matches, a small bell and snuffer are used in this healing meditation. The members of the healing group are seated in a circle and the facilitator begins the ceremony.

The Meditation

"Let us relax our physical bodies... quiet our emotions... still our minds... and harmonize our consciousness." (pause)

"By an effort of the will let us enclose our group in a sphere of white light." (pause)

"Let us think of ourselves as a chalice into which the Divine Light is poured. As we aspire to be one with this Life, the cup increases in size, growing ever stronger in the inner world, where dwells the Healing Life." (pause)

"Let us think of this Life, in all its glowing splendor, flooding us with its power, and flowing through our hearts to heal the sorrows and suffering of the world." (pause)

"Let us dwell in thought on the Christ Principle, as the source of healing power." (pause)

The facilitator rings a small bell and all stand.

The facilitator then lights the candle on the right

and says: "I light this flame as a symbol of the Christ, the Lord of Compassion." (pause) Then he/she lights the candle on the left and says, "I light this flame as a symbol of St. Raphael, the healing archangel." At this point, the chalice is uncovered and the names are removed from the box.

The members are again seated and the facilitator says, "In reverence, we invoke the cooperation of the angelic hosts and dedicate ourselves as channels for the spiritual healing of the world."

While remaining seated, the members of the group recite the following prayer:

Hail devas of the healing art! Come to our aid.
Pour forth your healing life into these persons.
Let every cell be charged anew with vital force.
To every nerve give peace.
Let tortured sense be soothed.
May the rising tide of life set every limb aglow,
As by your healing power, both soul and body are restored.
Leave with each an angel watcher, to comfort and protect,
Till health returns or life departs,
That he may ward away all ill,
may hasten the returning strength, or lead to peace when life is done.
Hail devas of the healing art!
Come to our aid.
And share with us the labors of this earth,
That God may be set free in humanity.

At this point, the facilitator slowly and clearly reads the names of each person and places each name in the chalice, while the group members remain silent and in meditation.

After a pause, the facilitator extinguishes the candles and covers the chalice with the cloth. He/she says: "Let us turn our thoughts to the Lord of Love and Compassion and to the angelic hosts in gratitude, recognizing our privilege in working with them." There is a pause, followed by short ringing of the bell.

The seated members of the circle join the facilitator and say: "We rededicate our lives, together with the added power we have received, to the service of the world in which we live." (pause)

The facilitator says "The healing service is ended" and all participants leave the room in silence.

Ritual to Invoke Christ's Healing Presence

Preparation

The room is prepared as in the previous meditation ritual, with the box, chalice and candles. In the front of the table on the right, a small picture of the Christ may be placed. A small cross can be placed behind the chalice. It is suggested that members of the healing circle enter quietly and be seated in silence for several minutes before the meditation begins.

The Meditation

The facilitator begins the ceremony, speaking slowly and clearly:

O Gracious lord, we enter Thy radiance,
and approach Thy presence, bearing with us

107

the service done in Thy name and for Thee. We seek to become more efficient servers, and we open our hearts and minds to the power of Thy Love, and Thy Joy, and Thy peace.

May Thy Love flood our beings; Thy Love which is gentleness, kindness, helpfulness. We wish to be loving, kind and helpful to all our brothers and sisters.

May Thy Joy pervade us; Joy which is Light, Radiance, Eternal Youth. We wish to bear Thy Joy to those who are sad, lonely and depressed.

May Thy Peace enfold us and fill us with contentment, certainty, rest, stillness; Thy Peace which passes understanding. We wish to be a center of Love, Joy and Peace in the World.

We place all our love and trust and confidence in Thee, for Thou are the Lord. From the unreal, lead us to the real; from darkness, lead us to light; from death, to Life Eternal.

At Thy feet and in Thy Light, we strive to realize who we are. We are not these bodies which belong to the world of shadows; we are not the desires which affect it; we are not the thoughts which fill the mind; we are not the mind itself.

I am the Diving Flame within my heart, eternal, immortal, ancient, without beginning and without end; more radiant then the Sun in all its noonday glory, purer than the snow, untouched and unsullied by the hand of matter; more subtle than the ether is the spirit within my heart. I worship thee, I adore Thee, Thou art my life, my breath, my being, my all.

Lead me, O Gracious Lord, through Thy limitless Love to union with Thee and the Heart of Eternal Love.

After a pause, a bell is sounded and all stand.

The facilitator lights the candle on the right and says: "I light this flame in the name of the Christ". After a pause, he/she lights the candle on the left, saying "I light this candle in the name of St. Raphael." After a pause, the facilitator removes the cover from the chalice and takes the names out.

The group is seated and the facilitator says the following: "Let us dwell in thought upon the Christ Presence, Great Healing Life of the world, and the source of Healing Grace."

After a pause, all present recite the following prayer:

Oh Lord of Life and Love
Teacher of angels and humanity
We invoke Thy Mighty Power in all its
splendor;
Thy undying Love in all its potency;
Thy infinite Wisdom in all its perfection;

That they may now flow through us in a
relentless flood.
May the strengthening force of Thy life vibrate
through this channel;
The radiant light of Thy Wisdom shine
through this channel;
The healing power of Thy Love pour through this
channel.

The facilitator reads each name, and places it into the chalice. He/she then says: "Eternal rest grant unto these, O Lord, and may perpetual light shine upon them." After a pause, the bell is sounded. The facilitator then extinguishes the candles and covers the chalice once more.

The group members recite the following prayer:

O Lord of Love and Compassion, who gave the
promise that where two or three are gathered
together in Thy name, Thou would be in their
midst, grant us to be channels of Thy Love to
the world, pure instruments for Thy service, to
awaken the souls of women and men to the
knowledge of Thy Healing Presence.   Amen.

After a pause, the facilitator says: "The healing meeting is closed" and all members leave the room in silence.

Outdoor Meditation to Aid in Transforming Feelings

The following meditation exercise is based on a sacred exercise taught by Sun Bear, a Native American shaman and founder of the Bear Tribe. It was designed to help us release negative feelings (often involving pain, anger and frustration) and send them to the Earth Mother for healing and transformation.

Go to an isolated place in the forest, preferably out of earshot of surrounding homes and businesses. Ideally the area can be a place where you can lie down comfortably on your stomach.

While standing or sitting in a cross-legged position, spend several minutes doing one of the Basic Relaxation exercises described earlier in this book. Try to feel your connection with the Earth Mother. After several minutes, say "Earth Mother, I pray to release my feelings and give them to You for healing and transformation."

Lying face down on the ground, feel free to scream, cry or yell in order to empty your being of any anger, fear, hurt, frustration or resentment you may have. Pound your fists on the ground if you wish (this is not a "dignified" meditation exercise). Allow your feelings to be expressed directly into the earth. At the same time, observe your train of thought and feelings as you allow them to be expressed without limiting or judging them.

When you are finished, return to a sitting or standing position (if possible) once more. Breathe deeply and feel your connection to the earth. Be aware of the healing power of the Earth Mother, your source of life and nurturing. Conclude your meditation with a prayer of thanks.

Tree of Life – Kabbalah Meditation

Among the early Jews, the date palm represented the symbolic Tree of Life in the Kabbalah, the ancient system of Jewish mysticism. The mystical tree of life, known as *Sephiroth*, is made up of the ten emanations of the infinite God, or the "qualities of God's infinity made manifest in a finite world."

Like the cosmic Asvatha tree of the Buddhists, the Sephirothic Tree is inverted, symbolizing the manifestation of the cosmos from a single transcendent source. Each of the ten *Sephira* represents a group of exalted ideas, titles and attributes, which we will list briefly as follows:

First Sephira: *Kether* (the crown or the primordial point)

Second Sephira: *Chokmah* (wisdom or the primordial idea)

Third Sephira: *Binah* (intelligence and understanding)

Fourth Sephira: *Chesed* or *Gedula* (Mercy or Love)

Fifth Sephira: *Geburah* (The "power" of God, chiefly manifested as Severity, strength, fortitude and justice)

Sixth Sephira: *Tipereth* (compassion, beauty, the heart and center of the Sephirothic Tree)

Seventh Sephira: *Netzach* (firmness, victory, or endurance)

Eighth Sephira: *Hod* (glory or majesty)

Ninth Sephira: *Yesod* (formation, or the foundation or basis of all active forces in God)

Tenth Sephira: *Malkuth* (the kingdom of earth, action, and all nature)

The Sephiroth is considered by kabbalists as a bridge connecting the finite universe with the infinite God. In the *Zohar*, a sacred compendium of kabbalistic teachings, it is said that the Torah is the Sephirothic Tree of Life and that all who occupy themselves with it are assured of life in the world to come.

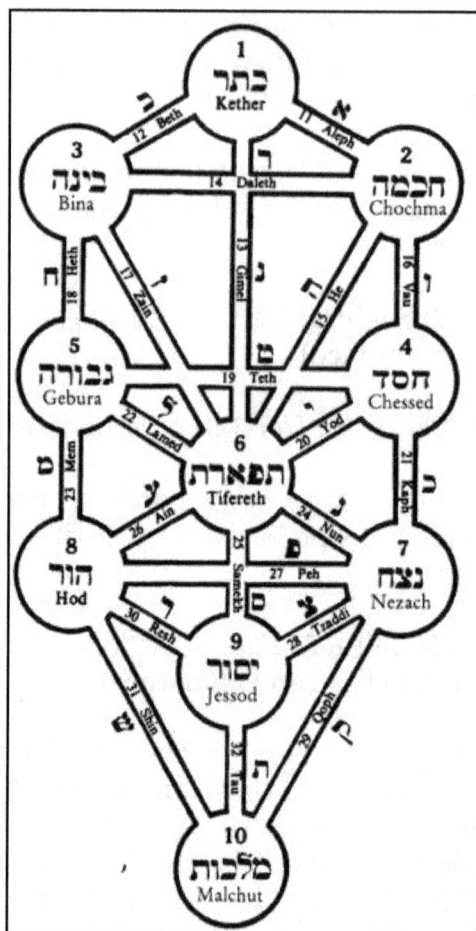

The Sephirothic Tree of Life
(with captions in Hebrew and German)

The Meditation

Before beginning this meditation, you may wish to light a white votive candle.

    1. Do one the Basic Relaxation exercises described earlier.

    2. Have before you an image of the Sephiroth. Choose one of the Divine Attributes, close your eyes, and ponder on it for several minutes. You may choose an attribute each day according to your intuition, or meditate on a different attribute daily in numerical order. During your meditation, allow your mind to make any associations or connections it needs to. At the conclusion of your meditation, record your observations in a journal.

Nature Meditations

Nature is a powerful source of beauty and inspiration, and meditating in a natural setting can be an unforgettable experience. However, even if we cannot meditate in a natural setting, we can create a visualization of Nature in our minds. The following meditations are devoted to exploring our connection with the natural world, and using Nature's magic to facilitate inner healing and transformation.

A Meditation in Nature

Being in nature helps mobilize our five basic senses and stimulates our sixth sense, the intuition. When going into nature to meditate, choose a natural form that attracts you, such as a lake, a stream or other body of water, a tree, a flower, a cliff, a meadow, or a mountain. Using your senses of sight, hearing, smell, touch and (if appropriate) taste, "observe" the natural form. Breathe fully, yet without forcing your breath.

Close your eyes, yet continue to visualize the natural form in your mind's eye. As you breathe, be aware of any thoughts, feelings, memories or personal associations that might come up. Be especially aware of your feelings, without judging them one way or the other.

Slowly open your eyes and come out of your meditation. Devote several minutes to recording your impressions in a notebook. Conclude by giving thanks to the natural form that assisted you in your meditation practice.

The following meditations can be done indoors.

In the Apple Orchard

1. Sit comfortably in a chair or on a meditation mat on the floor. Do one of the Basic Relaxation exercises presented elsewhere in this book, or use another relaxation method of your choice. Be aware of your breathing.

2. After you have relaxed your body and mind, imagine yourself walking down a path towards an apple orchard.

3. Visualize the trees in the orchard bearing the ripest of fruit. Bees, butterflies and songbirds are everywhere. In the distance, you hear a rushing stream. Pause for a moment and listen to it.

4. Feel yourself being welcomed into the orchard by the bees, birds and the trees themselves. It's a magical feeling. Pause.

5. Imagine yourself bowing in honor of the tree, and express the greeting "Your life is one with mine." Pause.

6. Picture yourself picking an apple from the tree. Bring it to your chest and hold it up in front of you. Pause.

7. Imagine yourself biting into the apple. It is the most delicious and juicy apple you have ever tasted. Imagine the apple's essence awakening your taste buds before permeating your entire being, bringing you nourishment, cleansing and inner healing.

8. After several minutes, respectfully take leave of the orchard, and return to your normal state of consciousness. Take several deep breaths and stretch if you like. Slowly leave your sitting position.

By the River

1. As in the previous meditation, sit comfortably in a chair or on a meditation mat on the floor. Do one of the Basic Relaxation exercises presented elsewhere in this book, or use another relaxation method of your choice. Be aware of your breathing.

2. After you have relaxed your body and mind, place your focus on your heart. It is constantly pumping blood throughout your body, and is also the abode of your love.

3. Visualize your heart as a river of pure, clean water. On the shore of the river is an altar made up entirely of precious stones, including amethysts, emeralds, rubies and diamonds. Behind the altar are

beautiful tropical trees in full blossom. The blossoms are beautiful to behold and their aroma permeates all of your senses.

4. Visualize yourself seated within this beautiful scene feeling yourself as one with it. Your heart feels rich and abundant. It is the center of your life. Enjoy your visit here. Express gratitude to be able to enjoy such richness in your life.

5. After several minutes, respectfully take your leave, and return to your normal state of consciousness. Take several deep breaths and stretch if you like. Slowly leave your sitting position.

Meditations on the Four Elements

The purpose of these meditations is to allow us to deepen our connection with the four elements of the Earth: earth, fire, water and air. Although not necessary, these meditations are most successful when done outdoors in a natural setting.

Earth

As you sit comfortably or lie down on your back, devote several minutes to relaxation, using one of the Basic Relaxation exercises described earlier in this book. Pay special attention to your breathing. Visualize all your tension leave your body until you feel completely relaxed.

Feel your physical and energetic connection to the earth. Imagine that its strength is not only supporting you, but is giving you vital energy. Remember that the earth contains minerals, like iron, calcium, silica and magnesium that are also found in your body, so you have both an energetic and biochemical connection to the earth. Feel this connection and your gratitude towards the earth element as you continue to breathe deeply.

Fire

This meditation is best done on a sunny day (wear a hat or sunscreen as needed).

Sit comfortably or lie down on your back. As in the previous meditation, devote several minutes to progressive relaxation. Take full, deep breaths, knowing that you are bringing life force into your body with each incoming breath.

Feel the warmth and light of the sun on your body. The fire of the sun can destroy, but is essential for life and creation. As you breathe, focus on the essential qualities of life: heat, passion, purification. Feel the heat within your body, filling you with passion and inspiration. Know too that the fire element within your body allows your immune system to function, killing viruses, bacteria and germs with the purifying heat. Feel the fire within fill you with the energy to develop creative visions and achieve new goals. Feel your gratitude for the fire element in your life.

Water

Sit or lie down near a river, lake or other body of water. If this is not possible, sit near a fountain. A glass of water will do also!

As in previous exercises, devote several minutes to relaxation and deep breathing until you feel completely relaxed.

Visualize the element of water and the importance it has in your life. Ponder on its nourishing and purifying qualities. Think about the spiritual essence of water and flowing water as symbolizing the movement of life. Remind yourself that over 75 percent of your body is made up of water, and imagine how water functions in your organs, tissues and body processes, like circulation, locomotion, elimination and digestion. Visualize the water element bringing you cleansing and healing, and feel your gratitude towards it.

Air

This meditation is best done outdoors. Sit down comfortably on a chair or on the ground. Devote several minutes to deep, rhythmic breathing as described in one of the breathing exercises earlier in this book. Continue to practice deep breathing until you feel completely relaxed.

Focus your attention on the all-pervading qualities of air: the air that you breathe and that gives you the gift of life; the gentle breezes that caress your face, and the winds that bring new ideas and fresh perspectives.

Finally, feel your connection with the air element within- the oxygen that energizes and nourishes every cell of your body. As you breathe deeply of the life-giving air, feel your gratitude towards it.

Flower Meditations

In addition to their beauty, flowers are a potent source of inspiration and wisdom. They possess the ability to elevate our spirits, and bring us hope and comfort during times of difficulty. Many feel that the presence of flowers in a hospital room can help speed the patient's recovery.

Meditating with flowers can be a powerful experience that is both gentle and transformational. The following four meditations utilize the power of flowers in different ways. Remember that the first three meditations can be varied with different species of flowers, which will impart a different keynote quality to each meditative experience.

I.

Place a single flower in a vase and set it before you. If you do not have access to a fresh flower, a color photograph of a flower will do. This meditation can be varied with different types and species of flowers.

1. Perform one of the Basic Relaxation exercises described earlier.

2. Observe the flower carefully: its colors, textures, aroma and form.

3. After a few minutes of observation, gently close your eyes, imagining the flower in your mind's eye.

4. Think about what the flower means to you, both as a symbol and as a friend. As you observe your thoughts about the flower, be aware of other associations that may come to mind.

5. As the mental images of the flower begin to

fade, open your eyes again.

6. After a few minutes of observation, gently conclude your meditation.

II.

Pen and notebook in hand, go outdoors and quietly observe the flowers in your garden or neighborhood. Take your time and observe the flowers as though you were doing a walking meditation. Chances are that you will be intuitively drawn to one flower in particular; you may even feel that the flower itself it trying to attract your attention!

Quietly observe the flower. Pay attention to its form, color, aroma and "energetic presence" in the garden. Gently touch the flower if you wish to. Send the flower your good feelings. As another living being, the flower responds to your energy the same way you may respond to the flower. Devote several minutes to quiet observation.

Sitting down on the ground (if possible), perform one of the Basic Relaxation exercises. At this point, you can silently contemplate the flower with your eyes open. Or, if you choose, you can mentally ask the flower for a message that seems to resonate with your idea of the flower's essential "keynote quality," such as enthusiasm, delicacy, flexibility or strength. Very often, you may receive a mental impression from the flower concerning a matter of importance, or you can ask "Please teach me about healing" or "Please teach me about beauty." It may be a message you can write down in your notebook, or you may wish to draw the flower instead. Be calm and be open for any eventuality. Devote a maximum of ten minutes to this meditation exercise, especially at first.

III. A Healing Meditation with Flowers

1. Go to a garden or to some wild flowers in a field. It is important that you allow yourself to be drawn to the specific flowers you wish to work with today. Sit down comfortably on the ground. Devote several minutes to one of the Basic Relaxation exercises or choose another one that works for you until you feel comfortable and relaxed.

2. Silently observe the flowers. As you contemplate them, visualize the flowers beginning from a tiny seed deep in the earth. Imagine them breaking through the soil. Observe each flower's color, form and overall beauty. Feel the flower's strength and vitality; its utter joy to be alive and its ability to express itself to the fullest, even in a sometimes difficult environment. Allow yourself to connect with the energy of the flowers, both individually and as a group.

3. Take several deep breaths. Turn your focus back on yourself and your own physical and emotional condition. Note that both you and the flowers share the same life force that comes from the earth, which assures your survival, growth and healing. Know that the possibilities for healing are tremendous.

4. Offer a prayer like: "I pray for the power of nature to help me heal my life," or create one that applies more to your specific health situation. And allow yourself to feel inspiration and appreciation for the beauty around you. Devote at least ten minutes to this meditation, but end it if you feel tired.

5. Before concluding your meditation, take several deep breaths and stretch. Repeat this meditation as

often as you wish.

IV. Red Rose Meditation

The red rose is a powerful symbol of human love. Among the most valued of garden flowers, the rose is an enduring symbol of unfolding love. This meditation is related to the chakra meditations discussed elsewhere in this book; refer to the section discussing chakra meditations before you do this one.

1. Sit comfortably in a straight-backed chair or on a meditation cushion or mat.

2. Be aware of your breathing. Take slow, deep and even breaths. At each exhalation, feel the tension drain out of your body and mind.

3. When you feel fully relaxed, visualize your heart chakra as a pure, fresh rosebud ready to open.

4. Continue your breathing. Visualize the rosebud opening slowly. As it unfolds, pay attention to each individual petal as representing a quality of love. They may include compassion, caring, devotion, protection, passion, kindness, selflessness, service, caring or nurturing.

5. As your heart center continues to open, imagine your feelings of love radiating outwards into the world. As the rose opens, think of those whom you love and send them love at this time. Do not forget to include yourself as well. Allow at least several minutes for this part of the meditation.

6. While you continue to breathe, allow your heart feelings to expand their range as you radiate love to the larger community. See your heart as full and healthy, radiating love and light.

124

7. As you conclude your meditation, take several deep breaths, holding your hands on your heart center. After a few stretches, slowly get up from your meditation position.

Tree Meditations

Trees have always played a central role in the survival of humanity and in the flowering of myriad cultures, including the ancient Egyptians, Hebrews, Greeks, Romans, Indians, Japanese, Chinese and Native Americans. Although many of us consider trees to be inanimate objects that may be pleasant to look at, indigenous peoples have long considered trees as sacred beings that can offer wisdom, guidance, inspiration and healing.

Many believe that because humans and trees both live in the vertical dimension (although trees remain in one place throughout life while humans are constantly moving) we share a special bond of friendship.

The following meditations are designed to help us create a deeper connection with trees and open ourselves to their life-giving and life-affirming nature.

I. Receiving Guidance

Pen and notebook in hand, go outdoors and quietly observe the trees in a park or forest. Take your time and observe the trees as though you were doing one of the walking meditations described elsewhere in this

125

Linden Tree

book. Chances are that you will be intuitively drawn to one tree in particular; you may even feel that the tree itself it trying to attract your attention.

Quietly observe the tree at first, and then move slowly towards it. Carefully observe its form, leaves, and colors; also, be aware of its "energetic presence." Silently extend a friendly greeting to the tree, as you would when you meet a new human friend. As another living being, the tree responds to your energy the same way you may respond to it. Touch the trunk, the branches and leaves if you wish to; get to know the tree as another living being. Remember that humans and trees are chemically and biologically connected: in addition to providing us with food and medicine, trees provide us with the oxygen we need to survive. Express your gratitude to the tree for its gifts to humanity. Devote several minutes to quiet observation and communion.

Sitting comfortably on the ground (or on a bench if one is handy), perform one of the Basic Relaxation exercises. Silently contemplate the tree with your eyes open for a few minutes. At this point, you can make a choice regarding the direction of your meditation:

Holding the image of the tree in your consciousness, you can close your eyes and meditate silently for five to ten minutes. If your mind begins to wander, open your eyes and refresh your image of the tree. Pay attention to your breathing, and be aware of any thoughts or feelings that may come up regarding the tree and your relationship to it.

You can mentally ask the tree for a message. You may have a question or problem that you have difficulty with, or you can simply ask the tree for help in general. Record your impressions in a notebook. Be calm and be open for any eventuality. Devote a maximum of ten minutes to this meditation exercise, especially at first. If you feel a special connection to the tree, return often for additional meditation sessions.

Conclude your meditation with a brief expression of gratitude. Do several stretches and slowly rise from your meditation posture.

II. Meditations on Individual Tree Species

1. Go to a tree, or imagine yourself standing near a tree.

2. Stand comfortably erect, bending your knees slightly, making sure your knees are not locked. Feel your feet on the ground and the ground supporting your body.

3. Imagine a vertical line in the center of your being moving down from the sky through your spine, and continuing through both feet, penetrating the earth.

4. Breathe normally and with awareness of your breath.

5. Try to "feel" what it is like to be a tree (devote at least two minutes to each of the following exercises):

Oak Meditation

6. Feel your body strong and straight.

7. Hold your arms open at a 45-degree angle to your body, with palms turned upwards.

8. Feel yourself stable against the winds of life; while flexible and able to adapt to the challenges.

128

Affirm your groundedness in truth.

9. Visualize yourself as providing others with nourishment, strength and protection.

10. Feel your connection to both the earth and the sky, drawing both wisdom from the earth and nourishment from the sky and sun.

Pine Meditation

6. Feel your body strong and straight. Imagine your head to be higher than it actually is.

7. Hold your arms open at a 45-degree angle to your body, palms facing downwards.

8. Feel your connection to the earth.

9. Feel yourself solid yet flexible; with your boughs offering a blessing to those around you.

10. Meditate on the concept of compassion and see yourself as a source of understanding and compassion for others.

Gingko Meditation

6. Feel yourself as ancient as the Earth itself, going back to the time of the dinosaurs, unique and unconventional.

7. As an aged being from the East, acknowledge your ability to adapt and thrive, even in difficult circumstances.

8. Specifically acknowledge how you have succeeded in your life up to now, and how you persevered. What innate talents and abilities did you use to accomplish this?

9. See yourself as having succeeded while keeping your beauty and maintaining your individuality.

10. Finally, acknowledge that your challenges in your life are gifts from the Earth Mother that have strengthened you and have increased your power and resourcefulness.

Maple Meditation

6. Feel yourself as abundant and receptive, with your branches opening in all directions, reaching out to others.

7. Imagine your branches as a form of antennae, receiving information from the world around you.

8. At the same time, be conscious of how you affect others around you by your thoughts, feelings and actions.

9. Visualize yourself receiving the best from others and giving your best in return.

10. Finally, experience the joy of the maple tree; strong, bright and intimately involved with life around it.

Weeping Willow Meditation

6. Stand erect, with your shoulders relaxed and your arms at your sides.

7. Visualize yourself as a tree of calm and grace, even when you are experiencing difficulty in your life. You are grounded in reality and acknowledge the truth of your situation at the moment.

8. Now feel your strong connection to the water element with its inherent fluidity and nourishing properties; giving life to every cell of your body.

10. Acknowledge the water element as a part of you that is ever-present; at the same time, see yourself

as part of this eternal movement of life.

III. Acorn Meditation

After performing one of the Basic Relaxation exercises presented earlier in this book, take an actual acorn and hold it in your hand; if an acorn is not available, use a photograph or hold a mental image of an acorn in your mind's eye.

As you imagine the acorn, allow your mind to explore any associations the acorn has for you. Continue to be aware of your breathing.

If your mind moves too far afield from your subject, gently move your focus back to the image of the acorn.

After several minutes, conclude your meditation.

IV. A Healing Tree Meditation

Choose a large, healthy tree to which you feel drawn. Sit down either facing the tree, with your spine resting against it, or lie down with your feet touching (or almost touching) the tree. If you feel especially needful of support or of a physical connection to the tree, embrace the tree with your body pressed against it.

1. Devote several minutes to one of the Basic Relaxation exercises until you feel comfortable and relaxed.

2. As you breathe evenly and fully, feel your energetic connection with the tree. Like the tree, imagine yourself to be in total alignment in your body, mind and emotions. Feel the energy of the tree intermingling with yours. Feel the vital power of the tree strengthen your energy field and your feeling of

being "grounded" in the earth.

3. Ask the tree for healing. You can say something like, "Brother/sister tree, my life force is one with yours. Please help me to heal." Say this with feeling and sincerity, as though the tree were a dear friend who can truly assist you in the healing process.

4. Devote several minutes to receptive silence and contemplation. Allow yourself to be open to new (and sometimes unexpected) ideas, impressions and insights about your health situation and how you might improve it. Continue to breathe, taking slow, natural breaths. Feel your connection to the tree and its indwelling spirit of intelligence, love and power. Record your experiences in a journal if you wish.

5. After ten minutes, you are ready to conclude your meditation. Express your gratitude to the tree and slowly take your leave. If you feel that you have benefitted from this meditation, return to the tree again for additional healing sessions.

Water Meditations

Communing with the spiritual essence of water is not a difficult task. Select a lake, river or spring that you feel especially connected to, and approach the area with respect and quiet awareness.

After arriving at the watery spot, a short prayer is often appropriate, such as "I come to you in the spirit of oneness" or "We are both one with the Great Spirit." We can also ask the Water Element for help in accessing deeper insight and greater earth wisdom; we can request that what we are about to receive will assist us in the healing process, whether it be our own healing, or healing between ourselves and nature. Although we need to avoid standing outdoors in a thunderstorm, we can also commune with the spiritual element of water by asking the rain and wind for spiritual cleansing and to fill us with their power.

We can also recite traditional prayers familiar to us before meditating, such as *The Lord's Prayer*, the *Hail Mary*, the *Gayatri*, or another prayer of our choice. Prayers of praise to the Great Spirit or Universal Presence are especially useful in safely invoking the spiritual power of water, which will enhance our meditative experience.

This section contains some of my favorite water meditations. The first two can be done outdoors, while the other can be done in the home.

I.

Find a comfortable place where you can be quiet and alone, and select a comfortable position.

For those who prefer to meditate with eyes open, quietly observe the body of water; if you are meditating by the ocean, you might focus your gaze at a spot about twenty to thirty feet in front of you; if you are meditating by a waterfall, you can observe the water as it begins to fall from the summit, or at point midway on the water's cascade. This will keep your mind from wandering. If you prefer to close your eyes, try to visualize a field of white light while being aware of the natural sounds around you.

Begin to breathe slowly and deeply, becoming aware of your breath as it enters and leaves your body. Each time your mind wanders to other thoughts or is disturbed by outside noises, gently bring your attention back to the easy, natural rhythm of your breathing. If you have trouble keeping your mind on your breath, count each inhalation and exhalation up to ten, and then start over again.

As you relax physically, you may find that various feelings come and go. They shouldn't be repressed, but the very act of calmly observing them may cause the images and feelings to gradually lose their intensity.

Gradually intuit and then visualize the concept of oneness with the body of water you are observing. After several minutes, gradually expand your feelings of oneness to include all beings. Express your desire to experience the reality of oneness as an integral part of your life today, either in silence or out loud: "I pray to realize my connection with nature today." Repeat this visualization slowly several times. You can also express other desires or yearnings you have which you want to integrate into your life.

After having expressed your keynote visualization, relax and become receptive once more. Continue your relaxed, deep breathing for at least three minutes and feel the sense of oneness living inside your body, near the heart. Feel it streaming out towards the body of water, and further out into the world. Conclude your meditation gradually and in silence.

II.

Sit near a lake, stream, river or ocean. As you breathe quietly and evenly, observe the light reflecting on the water and see how the light is constantly changing. Observe the changing light. As you do, you see your mind alive and changing as well.

III.

Place a glass of water in front of you.

1. As you breathe, observe the water as essential to your life. Observe your mind as you explore the meaning that water has for you.

2. If your mind wanders, gently and patiently bring your focus back to the water. This part of the meditation can take several minutes.

3. As you continue your meditation, gently lift the glass and slowly drink the water, taking small sips at a time. Devote several minutes to ingesting the water. Be aware of any feelings as you do this.

Meditating on Numbers

The science of numbers can be traced to ancient Greece, Egypt and Assyria. Although primarily used as symbols of quantity, mystics and alchemists taught that numbers hold deeper, more subtle meanings. They can symbolize universal truths and specific aspects of creation.

Closely related is the art and science of numerology. Numerologists teach that each number reflects certain aptitudes and psychological characteristics. Each letter of one's name is given a numerical value and the sum of the numbers of your name and birth date is believed to offer important insights about our character, life task and hidden talents and abilities.

The following list contains some of the major keynote qualities of the numbers. You may relate other meanings to these numbers through personal experience, and you may discover more through meditation. Curiously, a number may be reflect a paradox, and contain two completely opposite meanings. For example, the number *0* symbolizes both infinitely large and infinitely small!

0 Infinity. Universality, totality; the cycles of life; the point at the center; the outer circumference, limitation.

1 Manifestation. Positive or active principle in nature, initiating action, pioneering, leading, selfhood, independence, rulership; God, primary; the fundamental unity of all things. Symbol of the Sun.

2 Antithesis (positive and negative, male and female, yin and yang): dualism (spirit and matter, implicit and explicit); unites opposite principles, cooperation, adaptability, mediating, combination, partnering. Symbol of the Moon.

3 Trinity (Father, Son, Holy Spirit; life, substance, intelligence; father, mother, child; force, matter, consciousness; past, present, future); extension of the self; expression, verbalization, socialization. Symbol of Mars.

4 The material universe: physical laws, logic and reason; cube or square; the intellect that can distinguish between the material and spiritual aspects of life; foundation, order, struggle against limits, slow yet steady growth. Symbol of Mercury.

5 Expansion, increase, fertility, reaping, harvest; reproduction of self in the material realms; the judgment. The symbol of Jupiter.

6 Cooperation, uniting, marriage, harmony, peace, resolution; reciprocal action, interaction between spiritual and material; alchemy. Symbol of Venus.

7 Completion: the seven days of the week, the seven basic colors, the seven human temperaments; cycle of evolution, time and space; analysis, understanding, knowledge, awareness. Symbol of Saturn.

8 Dissolution; laws of cyclic evolution, reaction, rupture, disintegration, separation; the incoming breath; genius; inventive; material goals. Symbol of Uranus.

9 Regeneration; travel, going forth, reaching out, giving, selflessness, extension; spirituality, extrasensory perception; new birth, creative expression. Symbol of Neptune.

The Method

1. Write down each number clearly on an index card to observe while you meditate. You also may want a pen and notebook for this meditation as well.
2. Sit in a comfortable position, either in a straight-baked chair or on a mat or cushion on the floor. Perform one of the Basic Relaxation exercises

described earlier.

3. Choose a number on which to meditate. With the different keywords of the number (listed above) in mind, ponder their meaning. What additional meanings does the number hold for you? How do you feel about the number? What significance does it have in your life? Allow your thoughts and feelings to come to the surface, and record them in your journal.

4. After ten minutes, slowly conclude your meditation exercise.

Walking Meditations

Most people believe that meditation is best practiced sitting down on a cushion or mat. Yet walking meditation can trace its roots back hundreds of years to the Zen meditation tradition.

Like the sitting meditations described earlier, meditation while walking helps the meditator to be aware. Yet unlike sitting, walking offers us a constant stream of images and experience that require ongoing observation.

I. Indoor Walking Meditation

For this meditation, you will want to create a clear path at least twelve feet (four meters) long. It is best to remove your shoes for this exercise so you can better feel your contact with the floor.

1. Begin by standing up, devoting several minutes to one of the Basic Relaxation exercises or other form of relaxation. Your body relaxed, bend your knees

slightly and "feel" your feet connected to the floor. Place your hands gently at your sides, or clasp your hands behind you. Remain conscious of your breathing.

2. Start walking slowly, looking down at the floor several feet ahead of you. Be aware as each foot touches the floor, as well as the forward movement of your body as you move. Your mind will constantly shift its focus as you apply each foot to the floor, place your weight on your foot, bend your knee, and move your other foot. Simply be aware of your movement, which should be gradual, fluid and easy.

3. When you reach the end of your indoor path, gently turn around. Be aware of your movements as you do this. Continue to observe your breathing, and be aware of any thoughts that may come up. If you find yourself daydreaming or being otherwise distracted, gently bring your focus back to your movement.

4. When you return to your starting point, conclude your walking meditation. Stand still for several minutes. Bend your knees slightly and be aware of your breathing, noting your inner calm and dignity as you stand.

II. Outdoor Walking Meditation (alone)

For this walking meditation, you will want to either go barefoot or wear light shoes or sandals. Choose a predetermined route that will be approximately 12 to 27 feet (4-9 meters) in length.

1. As you stand comfortably with your knees slightly bent, take a few moments to relax. As you watch your breathing, feel your feet firmly planted on

the earth.

2. Begin walking slowly, while looking down at the ground several feet ahead of you. Be aware of your foot as it touches the ground. Feel the living earth supporting your body as it moves.

3. When you reach the end of your path, stop, and then turn around slowly. Remain mindful of your movement, as well as your connection to the earth. Slowly return to your starting point, being mindful of your breathing, your movement and your connection to the earth.

4. When you return to your starting point, stand still for several minutes, knees slightly bent. Continue to be aware of your breathing, as well as the supporting earth beneath your feet. As in the previous indoor walking meditation, note your feelings of inner calm and dignity as you stand.

III. Outdoor Walking Meditation (accompanied)

This walking meditation requires a partner. Before you begin, you will need a blindfold. Your partner will gently lead you for a short walk on a route that you have both determined is safe.

1. Before you begin, devote several minutes to one of the Basic Relaxation exercises. As in the previous walking meditation, bend your knees slightly and feel your connection to the earth, which is supporting you totally.

2. Put on the blindfold and have your partner turn you around several times so that you lose your sense of direction. Take your partner by the arm and

have him or her silently lead you on a slow yet steady walk.

3. As the two of you walk in silence, be aware of your feelings and sensations, without repressing them in any way. If you feel fear, observe your fear and "breathe into the fear" as you walk. Be aware, too, of feelings of enjoyment, trust and surrender.

4. Devote several minutes to this walking meditation. After you return to your original starting point, stand quietly for several minutes, being aware of your breathing as well as any feelings that may come up.

5. After concluding your meditation, write your impressions in a journal or share your experience with your partner. Allow your partner to share his/her experiences with you as well!

IV. Seeing and Listening

We often go through life in a state of non-attention. In order to function more efficiently in today's modern world, we often block out sights and sounds we do not wish to deal with. As a result, we often isolate ourselves from the rhythms of life and limit our life experience.

Seeing

This simple meditation helps us cultivate the art of seeing.

Leave your home for a walk through your neighborhood; devote from thirty to sixty minutes to this meditation so you do not feel rushed. You may

141

decide to choose the same route as you might take on an ordinary day, but this time you will walk slowly (at about half your normal speed) and walk while paying close attention to everything in your range of vision.

In this walking meditation, you may wish to stop and observe a neighborhood tree, gaze at a flower by the roadside, or examine the shingles on a roof of a nearby house. You may pause to watch children playing, or silently observe shoppers as they enter and leave the supermarket. Simply allow these sights to enter your consciousness without repressing them or judging them in any way.

Continue on with your walk. Chances are that you will see many familiar things, but will view them in a refreshingly new perspective.

Listening

As in the previous meditation, walk in silence for thirty minutes to an hour. This may involve a walk in your neighborhood, in a park or by the seashore.

In this exercise, you are not to speak, but merely *listen*, so you may want to limit your interaction with others. Listen to the sounds of nature, traffic, music, people talking, construction, and the sounds of airplanes flying overhead. Try not to ignore or otherwise block out any sounds. If any sounds distress you, breathe deeply to regain your composure.

V. Calling to Gaia: the Earth Goddess

Take a walking meditation in nature. Be especially aware of your breathing as you walk slowly in a natural setting, like a hiking trail, a meadow or by the seashore. Be especially aware of how you breathe and how and where you place your feet. Be receptive to the world around you, including the sights, sounds, smells, temperature, the wind on your face and the rays of the sun.

When you feel intuitively that the proper moment has arrived, sit down in a comfortable place. After taking several easy, deep breaths, look around. Observe the rocks, trees, grasses, flowers, sky. Close your eyes, and continue to breathe deeply for several minutes. Holding the beauty of your surroundings in your mind's eye, feel yourself as part of the world around you.

Slowly chant the name *Gaia*, the Greek Earth goddess, over and over. Feel your love and reverence for her: the mother who loves you, supports you and sustains you. Know that you are one of her beloved children. Enjoy your state of connectedness while you continue to chant for several minutes.

Cease chanting, and in silence, be open to any ideas or impressions that might enter your consciousness. After several minutes, open your eyes and see the natural world around you. Take several deep breaths, and offer Gaia your thanks. Stand up slowly and stretch.

VI. A Silent Walking Meditation (group)

Walking in nature as part of a group can a highly rewarding experience. There are many types of group walking meditations, and they will often be determined by your natural environment. A moonlight meditation on a path through the forest or a walking meditation along the shore at dawn will be very different experiences. This meditation is often conducted by a facilitator who can gently lead the group in the meditation process.

1. Before starting, the group should come together in a circle, joining hands. After the facilitator offers a brief description of the program, members can quietly focus their consciousness on the unique experience they will have both as individuals and as a group.

2. With the facilitator leading the group, members walk in a single file at a slow to moderate pace.

3. Silence is observed as they walk. In this silence, each participant is invited to use all of their senses, especially sight, hearing and smell. Be aware of the trees, animals, and sky and feel your connection to them all.

4. Ideally, the group should have a pre-determined destination. This can be a stream, a lake, a large tree or forest clearing. Participants maintain their silence as they arrive at their destination.

5. The facilitator can lead a small ceremony at this site. Members of the group can join hands while sitting in a circle. Prayer, chanting, or other forms of ritual can be done here, or silence can be maintained throughout. The type of ceremony may vary according to the destination. For example, a tree meditation (see pages 125-132) can be especially powerful under a large oak or redwood tree, while a meditation exploring the mysteries of moving water is appropriate when you are visiting a lake or ocean shore. However, some people may prefer to be alone at this time, and find a personal spot for meditation, prayer or silent reflection.

6. After a pre-determined period of time (which

might last from fifteen minutes to an hour), the group can assemble once more. The participants return walking in single file, and in silence.

7. The group returns to their original place of departure. Again, holding hands, members have the opportunity to share their experiences and feelings about the meditation walk. A closing prayer by the facilitator or other members of the group may conclude the meditation.

T'ai Chi Chuan Meditation

T'ai Chi Chuan is a Chinese system of exercise and movement mediation developed hundreds of years ago by Taoist monks. The practice of T'ai Chi involves special breathing techniques and a set of eighty-one movements, which involve nearly every part of the body, including hands and fingers, feet and toes, and the buttocks and eyes. These movements are done very slowly with each movement flowing into the next, as if it were only one long, continuous movement.

Although to observers, it appears to be a very relaxed form of meditative movement, T'ai Chi involves tremendous inner focus and concentration. One of the major goals of this practice is to gather life energy, known as *chi*, into the lower abdomen, and distribute it freely to the arms, legs, and the rest of the body. This enables the body to achieve a balance of Yin and Yang energy, which is believed to enhance overall health and provide mental, emotional and spiritual harmony.

Medical research carried out both in China and the West has found that the regular practice of T'ai Chi

Chuan can lower stress and blood pressure, enhances respiratory capacity and increases oxygen delivery to body cells, improves immune function, improves digestion, and increases leg strength, enhances balance and reduces falls among the elderly. This is probably why millions of Chinese of all ages practice T'ai Chi on a daily basis.

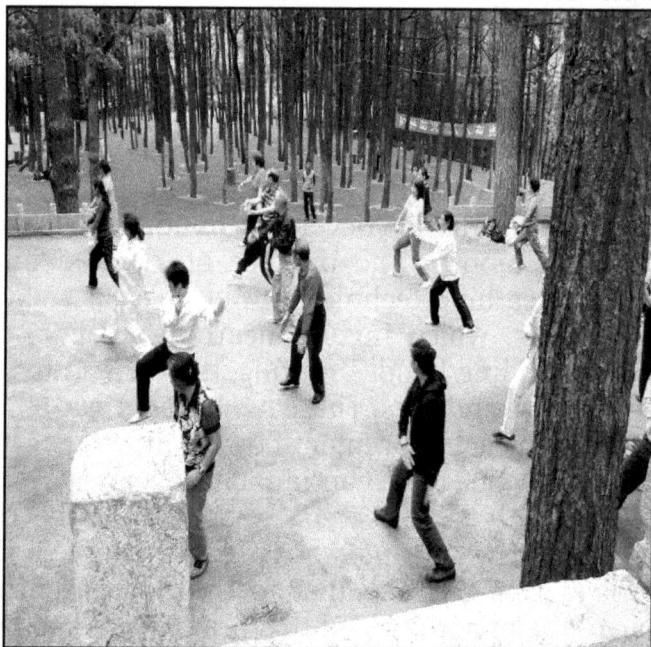

Morning T'ai Chi Exercise Class

Luolong Park - Kunming, China

An increasing number of Westerners choose T'ai Chi for their meditative practice, especially those who dislike meditating in a seated position. In addition to its tranquilizing effect on the emotions, T'ai Chi enables us to get more in touch with the life energy in the Universe and in our own body. T'ai Chi also helps us to conserve energy and produces a feeling of physical confidence and emotional security.

Like many martial arts, T'ai Chi cannot be taught from a book such as this one. However, a variety of videos are available for purchase in stores or online, or can be borrowed from many public libraries.

Classes in T'ai Chi are becoming easier to find in many cities and towns. In addition to specialized schools devoted to T'ai Chi itself, one can find instruction in martial arts academies, health clubs, the YMCA, meditation schools, senior centers and at adult education classes. High schools and universities often provide classes in T'ai Chi in their physical education programs or as an extracurricular activity.

Seeking Wisdom

In traditional cultures, community members often have access to a wise elder who is a source of instruction, comfort and advice. Often a shaman or medicine person, the elder is regarded as a type of community treasure, whose advice is highly valued by tribal members. In many cases, this person helps members of the community to access their own innate wisdom by telling stories or asking questions.

However, most of us today do not have access to a

wise and trusted older adult who can offer us clarity and vision when we are facing a difficult problem.

The following exercise is designed to help us access wisdom in our life by contacting "the sage within" through meditation.

1. Perform one of the Basic Relaxation exercises described earlier.

2. Close your eyes. Imagine that you are in the presence of a sage: a wise person of limitless knowledge and compassion. Know also that this person is very concerned about your welfare, and is happy to help you in any way possible. Imagine yourself making respectful contact with this elder.

3. Ask this person a question about an issue that has been troubling you: it may be a problem in your relationship, an important career decision you have to make, or a question about how you can improve your health. Continue to be aware of your breathing as you ask this question.

4. Allow yourself to be receptive to whatever response may come up. You may receive a direct answer, or you may be asked a question in return. Allow yourself to be open to whatever questions or answers you receive.

5. After several minutes, express gratitude to this person and take leave of him or her. Conclude your meditation.

6. Write down your experiences in a journal. Remember that you may not receive a final answer to your question in one session. It is possible that the information you received during your meditation may lead to additional questions to ponder before you arrive at a satisfactory solution. With practice, this

meditation can become an important learning tool.

Daily Review Meditations

As human beings, we are made up of a variety of often contradictory currents. We have qualities that we view as positive, like compassion, humor, courage and openness to new ideas. We also have qualities we label as negative, like jealousy, possessiveness, fearfulness and dishonesty. Very often, we tend to ignore the negative currents, or we downplay their significance in our lives.
It is not unlike having to deal with a noisy child who constantly demands our attention. We want them to leave us in peace and we may either ignore them or send them to their room. We often ignore our negative feelings or simply pretend that they do not exist.

Unfortunately, like the child who feels that he is being ignored by his parents, the negative feelings demand our attention with greater and greater intensity. When unresolved feelings are not dealt with directly, they often create situations in our life that force us to deal with them anyway. Very often these situations form a pattern. Though we often judge them as "bad," our difficulties can provide us with the stepping stones that enable us to make positive changes in our ways of thinking and feeling.

Spiritual teachers have told us that one of the goals of meditation is to explore what are known as "lower-self issues" in order to transform them into positive qualities. Like digging through a layer of mud and dirt in order to uncover a buried treasure, so must we dig through the "dirt" of our lower nature to discover our universal soul.

There are many ways to achieve this, including psychotherapy, body-oriented therapies like Rolfing, Breathwork, bioenergetics, Core Energetics, and other self-awareness techniques. Another way is through the Daily Review Meditation. On the following pages, we'll present several forms of the Daily Review Meditation. As reflected by their name, these meditations are most effective when done on a daily basis.

Evening Daily Review

The best time to do this daily meditation is when you are ready for bed. You may also wish to do it whenever you are having trouble sleeping due to worry or another form of emotional disturbance. In order to perform this meditation, you should have a notebook or journal on hand, as well as a quiet place where you can be alone.

1. Sit quietly for several minutes at the end of your day. Take several deep, gentle breaths and affirm that you wish to explore areas of your being that have caused you difficulty during the day. You may make a prayer of your own, or simply "I pray to explore areas of my being that have caused me difficulty today."

2. After several minutes of receptive silence, write down keywords or sentences describing situations or feelings that caused disharmony in your life during the previous day. Be completely honest and candid in your statements, which are intended to be shared only between you and God. "I lost my temper with my wife today" or "I spread gossip about my co-worker today" would be two examples.

Such statements may reveal resentment, jealousy, anger, sadness, feelings of low self-esteem, or acts of deception towards yourself or others. Although you may feel ashamed about these feelings or actions, write them down anyway. They are all part of you and make up part of your internal "family."

Be careful not to judge yourself, nor make them worse than they really are. Remember that even the most uncomfortable or shameful situation can serve as a stepping stone to spiritual fulfillment.

3. Continue to write for seven to ten minutes. Be mindful of how your thoughts, feelings and actions caused disharmony during the day. When you've finished writing, say "I ask God [or the Great Spirit] to help me transform areas of disharmony within my being."

4. Over the days and weeks that you do this meditation, you will notice that there clear patterns that often reveal themselves. Ask yourself:

"How do they appear?"
"When do they come up and with whom?"
"How do they cause disharmony in my life?"
"What role do I have in creating this inner disharmony?"
"How can I change these negative currents?"

5. Over weeks and months of regular meditation, you will become more aware of both the geography and the dynamics of your lower nature. You will also find that you have become aware of many of the subtle tricks that were used to avoid recognizing and dealing with difficult issues. By bringing disharmonious issues to light, you find that you can work with them more

effectively, and transform negative currents into positive qualities that bring inner peace and greater awareness. Continue to ask God [or your Higher Self] for help with any area in your life that continues to cause you difficulty.

Morning Daily Review

Like the Evening Daily Review, many people who enjoy writing can practice a simple morning meditation that can help achieve greater harmony and awareness during the day.

1. Sit quietly for a few minutes, taking regular breaths.

2. Ask God or your Higher Self for help in exploring areas that are of concern to you as you begin your day.

3. While in a receptive state, simply write down phrases or key words that describe feelings of disharmony or concern. These may have to do with your feeling anger towards another person, anxiety about an interview at work, or fears about money or health. As in the Evening Daily Review, simply write down whatever comes up without making judgments about them. Write for seven to ten minutes.

4. Read what you have written down. Ask God or your Higher Self to help you become more aware of these issues during the day, and ask for help in transforming them from a place of intelligence and higher understanding.

As you explore these issues at the beginning of every day, you can relate to them with greater clarity and purpose. Over time, you will see that this morning meditation will allow you to understand the inner meaning of troublesome issues, and how they can be a catalyst for achieving spiritual growth and inner peace.

The Golden Stairs

The Golden Stairs is a series of guidelines that were offered to spiritual disciples by Madame Helena Petrovna Blavatsky (1831-1891), co-founder of the Theosophical Society and author of the metaphysical classics *Isis Unveiled, The Secret Doctrine* and *The Voice of the Silence.*

This meditation is best experienced as a member of a group, followed by group discussion. It can also be done alone.

Group members sit comfortably, either in straight-backed chairs or on mats placed on the floor.

After several minutes of deep breathing and progressive relaxation, the group intones the sacred word "OM" three times.

The facilitator reads: "May we, both individually and as a group, focus our thoughts on The Golden Stairs."

Each "stair" is then read slowly and clearly, followed by a pause of approximately one to two minutes.

Members of the group ponder on the meaning of each statement and how it can be reflected in their personal lives.

153

A clean life,
an open mind,
a pure heart,
an eager intellect,
an unveiled spiritual perception,
a brotherliness for all,
a readiness to receive advice and
instruction,
a courageous endurance of personal
injustice,
a brave declaration of principles,
a valiant defense of those who are unjustly
attacked,
a constant eye to the ideal of human
progression and perfection which the
Brahma Vidya [sacred science] depicts.

This is followed by the statement, "These are the golden stairs up the steps of which the learner may climb to the Temple of Divine Wisdom."

After several minutes of silence, the meditation is concluded with the chanting of the word "OM" three times.

Meditations on The Seven Rays

The ancients taught that humanity is made up of seven basic temperaments, which are also known as *The Seven Rays*. Each ray has a specific keynote quality, such as power, love, creativity, healing or inspiration. In most individuals, a single quality or ray tends to predominate, although elements of all the rays are believed to be part of every one of us.

This meditation is designed to allow us to develop a deeper understanding of human psychology through the Seven Rays, and allow them to manifest in positive ways in daily life.

The following list includes the type of person who embodies this ray, the core or keynote qualities of each ray, and the positive and negative psychological expressions of the ray itself.

First Ray

Type: soldier, ruler, leader
Core qualities: power, will, leadership, courage
Positive aspects: powerful, strong, brave, self-reliant
Negative aspects: domineering, power hungry, rigid, selfish

Second Ray

Type: teacher, healer, sage
Core qualities: universal love, wisdom, cooperation, intuition
Positive aspects: wise, loving, intuitive, generous
Negative qualities: sentimental, impractical, unwise self-sacrificing

Third Ray

Type: philosopher, scholar, banker, strategist
Core qualities: creative ideation, interpretive intelligence, comprehension

155

Positive aspects: adaptable, tactful, dignified, impartial
Negative aspects: indecisive, aloof, unsupportive, deceitful

Fourth Ray

Type: artist, mediator, interpreter
Core qualities: beauty, harmony, balance, stability, drama
Positive aspects: harmonious, artistic, lover of beauty
Negative aspects: self-indulgent, conceited, fickle

Fifth Ray

Type: scientist, mathematician, lawyer
Core qualities: analysis, logical, patience
Positive aspects: seeker of truth, patient, methodical, curious
Negative aspects: critical, pedantic, self-centered, closed- minded

Sixth Ray

Type: mystic, saint, devotee, evangelist
Core qualities: devotion, loyalty, one-pointedness
Positive aspects: loyal, devoted, selfless, inspirational
Negative aspects: fanatical, intolerant, narrow-minded

Seventh Ray

Type: priest, magician, politician,
ceremonialist
Core qualities: grace, order, chivalry, skill
Positive aspects: orderly, skillful,
detail-oriented, precise
Negative aspects: loves trappings of power
and office, uses others, regimented,
extravagant

In this meditation, you will choose a ray on which to
focus.

1. After doing one of the Basic Relaxation exercises
presented earlier, take several minutes to consider the
keynote qualities of the ray.
2. Ask yourself if you know someone (whether a
relative, friend or historical figure) who personifies the
quality of the ray to you. Pause.
3. Ask yourself questions like, "How do I relate to
the energy of this ray?" "How do I feel about the
meaning of this ray?" "How to I manifest it in my daily
life?" Think about both the positive and negative
expressions of the energy of each ray. Pause.
4. Allow your thoughts and feelings to surface
when you think about these issues, and write them
down in your journal. Try not to repress or judge your
responses.
5. Ask how you might manifest the positive
aspects of each ray in your life. Pause and wait for a
response. Write your impressions in your notebook.
6. After ten minutes, gradually conclude your
meditation.

157

Hawk Meditation

Visualization in meditation can be very helpful in seeing our problems from a different perspective. The following meditation is designed to enable us to view aspects of our life with greater clarity and vision.

1. After devoting several minutes to one of the Basic Relaxation exercises, imagine seeing a hawk soaring high above you. Observe how it takes advantage of the air currents as it glides effortlessly far above the earth.

2. Now visualize yourself as this hawk, and imagine the perspective you enjoy from such a high point in the sky.

3. Think of as problem that you have been dealing with.

4. From the hawk's perspective of distance and freedom, think about how you can deal with this issue. Gently explore the possibilities with awareness and dispassion. Devote at least five minutes to this part of the exercise.

5. Now gradually come back to earth, feeling refreshed and clear-headed.

6. Acknowledge any perspectives you may have gained.

7. Breathe gently for several minutes as you conclude your meditation.

8. Write your insights in a journal if you wish to do so.

Visiting the Mansion

The following meditations are designed to enable you do explore your "inner being" with ease and safety. They can be performed after doing one of the Basic Relaxation exercises described earlier.

I.

1. Imagine yourself in a beautiful mansion, with many rooms and doors. Some rooms of the mansion are warm and friendly, while others have been abandoned and forgotten. As you walk the hallways, you see a door with your name on it.

2. Reciting a small prayer of your choice for protection, you open the door. As you enter the room, imagine yourself to be crossing a threshold.

3. Be aware of your breathing as you quietly explore the room, examining its textures, colors and furnishings. Is it cold? Is it stuffy? Are the windows open? What do you like about the room? What makes you uncomfortable about it?

4. Stay with your feelings as you breathe. You feel grounded and safe as you observe the room.

5. After several minutes, mentally imagine yourself leaving the room, returning to the hallway of the mansion once more.

II.

1. Imagine yourself in a beautiful mansion, with many rooms and doors. Some rooms of the mansion are warm and friendly, while others have been

abandoned and forgotten. As you walk the hallways, you see a door with your name on it.

2. Reciting a small prayer of your choice for protection, you open the door. You find a spiral staircase leading downstairs. Slowly descend the staircase, being aware of the stairs, the texture of the walls, the light. Be aware of how you feel as you slowly move down the stairs. Don't judge your feelings; just observe them.

3. After a few minutes, acknowledge that it is time to leave. Reverse your journey up the stairs, until you stand outside the door.

"Getting to Know Your Potential Self" Meditation

Sit in a comfortable, straight-backed chair. Adjust your body so it can be in a comfortable position with your spine straight, your palms on your thighs facing up, and your feet flat on the floor.

Slowly close your eyes and start to breathe slowly, deeply and rhythmically.

Continue to breathe deeply as you count from one to ten. The higher the number, the more deeply relaxed you become.

"One"

"Two"

"Three"

"Four"

Feel the energy pulsate through your body, as you watch your breath.

"Five"

"Six"

"Seven"

You feel that the boundaries of your body are gently disappearing.

"Eight"

"Nine"

"Ten"

Your mind is awake while your physical body is at rest.

Now imagine that your mind has expanded beyond the boundaries of your body. It is free from physical tension and body limitations. You can now experience profound insights and life-transforming breakthroughs.

Using all your senses, including sight, smell, hearing, touch, and taste, imagine that you are standing in a meadow near a flowing stream. You feel very comfortable here. There are flowers everywhere. An orchard is in the background, and the trees are all in full bloom. Birds are singing. Bees and other insects are humming. You can hear the sound of water splashing on the rocks, and you can smell the spring flowers. The sky is blue, the air is crisp, and you feel a slight breeze on your face.

What do you see? What colors are there? What do you smell? What sounds do you hear? What do you feel touching you? What emotions do you feel? Experience the peace that is here.

As you are in this place of peace and beauty, imagine that you see a friendly figure approaching you. As you observe, imagine that the person coming toward you is *you* at your fullest potential. What qualities do you have within that are manifested in your life now? What do you look like? What qualities does that person have that you have not yet expressed in your life? Feel the kindness, the strength, and the enthusiasm that this person has as he or she is walking towards you.

What is the chosen life path of the individual walking towards you? What qualities has he/she developed? Breathe gently and continue to observe this person.

Imagine that this person has a message to share with you. What is the message? Can you open your ears to hear it? Hear it now.

Finally, imagine this person walking up to you, and make eye contact. See the love and understanding in the eyes of your realized self. Acknowledge your connectedness and love for each other.

Now slowly begin counting down from ten to one.
"Ten"
"Nine"
"Eight"
"Seven"
You feel both inner calm and a deep connection to your true self.
"Six"
"Five"
"Four"
"Three"
"Two"
"One"

When you reach "one" you will be wide awake both physically and mentally. You feel rested, relaxed and alert. You feel both inner calm and a deep connection to your true self.

Remember that through this meditation, you can come back anytime you want to enjoy the peace of this place and commune with your full potential self.

Chakra Meditations

In Hindu and Buddhist traditions, it is taught that our bodies contain seven "energy centers." Each energy center is called a *chakra*. The term itself comes from the Sanskrit, and means *wheel*. Each chakra is a swirling center of energy exchange, and has a specific role to play in our lives. Both ancient and modern proponents of these traditions teach that we possess seven major chakras, which correspond with seven glands or organs that are part of this system of exchange, as seen on the following page.

We need to understand the functions of chakras because they often respond to our attitudes and feelings, and in turn affect us in both subtle and not-so-subtle ways. When a chakra is open, it will either receive or transmit energy. The type of energy transmitted or received corresponds to the qualities represented by the specific chakra. When the chakra is blocked or otherwise closed, we are cut off from the particular energy the chakra brings to us.

By becoming more aware of where they are located and how they function, we can better understand the often hidden factors which affect the way we think and feel. We also can have a clearer idea of how we relate to others and why others relate to us as they do. Through patience and understanding, we can consciously work to gradually open these energy

163

centers, thus bringing about greater balance and harmony in our lives and relationships.

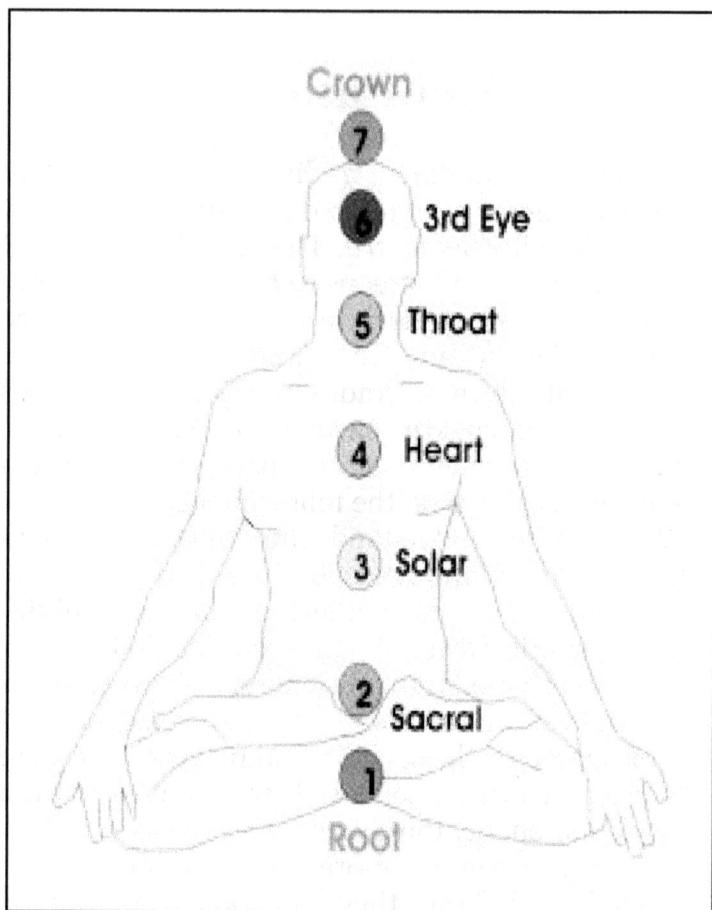

The Chakras

The Root Chakra

The *root chakra* is located at the base of the spine. It is the energy center that is related to our quantity of physical energy as well as our will to live. The root chakra is the seat of the Kundalini, which is also called "The Serpent Fire." It is a powerful force that exists on all planes and by means of which the rest of the chakras are aroused. When the life force or Kundalini is fully functioning through this center, the person has a strong ability to deal with physical reality. They are "grounded" in the world. However, when this chakra is blocked, the individual will experience a low level of physical vitality, and will probably not make a strong impression in the world.

The Sacral Chakra

The *sacral chakra* is located in the area of the body near the navel. It is connected with the sexual glands, and regulates both the amount and the quality of our sexual energy. When this chakra is open, it provides us with a strong sex drive and a correspondingly strong desire for sexual union. Just before we consciously find ourselves sexually excited, we often experience a "tingling" feeling in the sacral area. This is the sacral chakra getting ready for action.

When this chakra is blocked due to emotional problems or negative attitudes, our entire sex life is depressed, and the sexual act has little physical appeal. Women who have a severe block in this chakra are unable to achieve orgasm, and often find penetration painful. Men are prone to experience chronic impotence, premature ejaculation or general disinterest in sex if this chakra is blocked.

The Solar Plexus Chakra

The third energy center is known as the *solar plexus chakra*, which is located in the diaphragm region towards the center of the body. This chakra governs our feeling nature, and is closely linked to our emotions.

If we have an open solar plexus center, we enjoy a rich emotional life. When it is blocked, we often cannot "feel" emotionally. In many cases, a block in this chakra can cut off the energy flowing from the sacral chakra to the heart chakra, which makes us feel "cut off" from our partner during sex. When this occurs, sex will not be connected to love, and love feelings will not contain a sexual component.

This chakra is also connected to instinctual perception. When we speak of having "gut level feelings," we are describing one of the functions of the solar plexus chakra.

The Heart Chakra

The fourth chakra, or *heart chakra* is located in the center of the chest near the thymus gland. It is the energy center through which we love, and through which we can see the inner beauty of others. To the degree that this center is open and functioning, we have the ability to love our mates, our parents, our children, and our friends. Because this chakra is the home of romantic love, selflessness and compassion, it is the most important of our energy centers to develop at our present stage of evolution.

When we experience deep feelings of love, we sometimes can feel a type of "flutter" in the heart region. This is the heart chakra. And when we lose a loved one, we often feel pain in the heart area. When this occurs, the heart chakra may actually be wounded, and its functioning can be impaired. The term "to die of a broken heart" is believed by some observers to be more than a literary reference.

When this chakra is closed or blocked, the individual has problems loving others. People with a blocked heart chakra are often cold, calculating, and rarely give without expecting something in return.

The Throat Chakra

The fifth chakra is the *throat chakra*, whose location corresponds to that of the thyroid gland. The throat chakra is seen as primarily a receptive energy center, and is related to the power of *clairaudience* or psychic hearing. Through this chakra we receive impressions from the world around us: if our view of the world is positive, we will receive nourishment through this energy center. However, if our perceptions are negative, we will attract negativity. When this chakra is closed or blocked, we have difficulty "taking things in" whether they are new observations, unfamiliar ideas or the feelings of others.

The throat is also considered the active creative center. The words we speak- even in ordinary conversation- create our experiences, which can range from the most superficial (as with idle gossip) to the most profound. It is also the higher sexual chakra for humanity of the future, where our verbal exchange will be a major source of human creativity. In fact, the power of the word may even become as important as the physical exchange that takes place between two people when they make love at the present time.

The Brow or "Third Eye" Chakra

The sixth chakra, the *brow* or *"third eye" chakra*, is located on the forehead between the eyes. Because it is often related to clairvoyance, it is called "the third eye." This energy center is linked to the capacity to visualize and understand mental and spiritual concepts. When it is blocked or weak, the individual is often confused, and can have false images about the reality of things. There may also be blocks in forming creative ideas. Clairvoyants and holistic healers believe that the abuse of drugs -especially over long periods of time- affects the functioning of this chakra in a very negative way.

The Crown Chakra

The seventh and most powerful energy center is known as the *crown chakra*, which is located at the top of the head. When we have developed this chakra, we have reached perfection of all our faculties, and have a direct link between the lower and higher planes of existence.

The crown chakra symbolizes the connection to spirituality and the integration of our entire being on all levels, and as a result is fully energized by only spiritual masters and sages. This is where we remain connected to our soul and is why the infant has a soft spot on the top of the head. As the child develops a sense of identity with the physical body, this spot gradually hardens during the first year of life.

Energy Centers and the Serpent Power

All of the energy centers we've just described are given the power of life by the creative force in the universe, known in India as the *Kundalini*. Often called the "fire of passion," Kundalini is the fire energy in nature and stands behind all creativity and passion. We take this life force into our bodies with every breath we take. We also take in this life force by eating fresh, raw foods.

Of all the elements, fire symbolizes transformation: it takes something material and transforms it into another form. Through fire, materials are transformed into ashes and energy. The energy that is released by the fire doesn't cease to exist, but is transformed into something else.

In our own bodies, we are constantly transforming this universal energy and are utilizing it in hundreds of different ways. We use the creative force not only to keep our bodies alive and moving, but we use it to eat, to paint, to walk down the street, to work, to heal, to meditate, to make love. This is why metaphysics teaches that the fire energy or Kundalini is a magical element with the unique power to transform.

The Kundalini is also called the "Serpent Power" and is described in esoteric literature as a serpent lying dormant in humanity. It is often pictured as curled up at the base of the spine, the home of the root chakra. The serpent is a potent symbol of transformation, because it has the ability to shed its skin. The serpent most often represented in Buddhist literature is the cobra. Through its lethal bite, it can take other life forms from the physical world and

169

usher them through the portals of death to another dimension. Death is thus seen as a form of transformation.

Many ancient rituals (especially in the Tantra Yoga tradition) were devoted to awakening this serpent power so that it can gradually rise up through the spine. As it rises, this serpent power energizes the various chakras of the body until it finally opens and awakens the spiritual centers in the head. When the Kundalini force rises to higher chakras in our evolutionary process, we enter a new state of consciousness. We "die" to the old and embrace the next level of consciousness through this process of spiritual transformation.

Our energy centers are the voices in our development in the evolutionary process. In the early stages of our evolution, we function only from the root chakra, which is the primitive person seeking only survival. We sound only one note. As we evolve and grow, the higher chakras are energized one by one. In time, as the Kundalini rises to higher chakras, we gradually become a melody of many notes, with their accompanying power and splendor.

When developed with care and awareness, the chakras provide energy, balance and self-awareness. However, when they are stimulated artificially through drugs or through the unguided practice of certain types of Tantra yoga, they can be awakened prematurely by the Kundalini force. This often brings the person more energy than he or she can handle, and leads to imbalance on both physical and psychological levels. In extreme cases, it can result in insanity and even death.

For these reasons, it is very important to develop

the chakras in order beginning with the root, because it is necessary to have a strong foundation to support awareness in the next chakra. You cannot put a roof on a house with no walls and a weak foundation because the roof (and the entire house) will collapse.

In addition, the chakras must be continually balanced so that they are exchanging energy with each other, thus keeping all channels of communication open to prevent imbalances, and allow us to utilize a strong chakra to support and heal a weaker one. Techniques like aura balancing and polarity therapy, which relax certain chakras while stimulating others, help us achieve a balance of energies throughout both our dense and subtle bodies.

As we meditate on the energy centers of the body, we arrive at a deeper understanding of how each of them functions in our own life. We can ask "Where am I blocked?" "Where am I over-stimulated?" "What qualities do I need to develop which will bring about greater balance and harmony within?"

Meditations for Awakening the Chakras

I.

Form a triangle with your hands using the two forefingers and two thumbs. Hold this triangle over the chakra you wish to stimulate. Visualize or feel a pulsating white light in the chakra inside this triangle. Repeat the sound "HUM" over and over, which will focus and stimulate the energy within.

The apex of the triangle should point down at the root, sacral and solar plexus chakras to ground and stabilize the energy of this white light. When working with the higher chakras, the apex of the triangle should point upwards to inspire and uplift the light in the triangle.

When you do this exercise, begin at the root chakra and move upwards to the crown chakra. After you have sent light into this energy center, move your way back down to the root chakra once more.

II.

This is a more advanced meditation that works best with those who have already had some practice with meditation and visualization.

As you sit in a meditative posture, gently breathe in the Kundalini energy of the universe through the nose. Feel the breath go to the root chakra. Focus the breath there as you visualize a point of red energy. It is a single flame of hot, primal, dynamic power which will burst into activity in the higher chakras. Let your breath out again.

Now breathe in gently and focus at the sacral chakra. Visualize two colored points (red on the right and blue on the left) which will then form a line of purple light. This symbolizes their procreative dominion over the Earth, and the union of the active and receptive, the yin and the yang.

Now focus your breath on the solar plexus. Visualize three points in the form of a triangle surrounding this chakra. The top point is yellow, and the base points are both red. See these colors merge to form the color orange. This figure symbolizes courage and illumination for action with understanding. It also empowers our feelings with joy and innocence.

As we move to the heart chakra, we visualize a diamond. This diamond contains four points of blue. These four points symbolize compassion towards oneself and others, receptivity to love, wisdom in our attractions, and sensitivity to our needs and those of others in an equal balance of giving and receiving.

Let us now move to the throat chakra. As we visualize this energy center, we see a five-sided pentagon with two yellow points in the middle and three blue points surrounding them. These points create a field of green which symbolizes our verbal creativity. Through positive thoughts and words, we create our experiences of learning, healing, prosperity and expansion.

We now proceed to the brow chakra, the home of insight and intuition. As we breathe in, we visualize a splendid six-pointed star. Each opposite point on the star contains one each of the three primary colors. In your mind's eye, see these colors merging into the color indigo. This indigo star helps us to open the intuition, stimulate mental clarity, and bring wisdom to our thoughts. It is a vision of unity as we see our true position in the universe. We are an integral part of a unified whole.

We finally reach the crown chakra. As you gently breathe in and visualize this chakra, imagine it as a clear quartz crystal with all seven colors of the rainbow emanating through it. The crystal also radiates a yellow glow of both joy and understanding of our soul union and purpose.

Rainbow Color Meditations

Color is a form of vibrating energy that can affect the way we think and feel: colors can depress us, enable us to feel more optimistic; they can even help stimulate the immune system by their subtle actions on the human mind. We all know that walking into a room painted robin's-egg blue, for example, will produce a different feeling from a walking into a room painted bright red. Yet by using color consciously, we can help bring about major changes in all areas of our life.

The following meditations help us to access the hidden powers of color and the power that they can bring to our lives on physical, psychological, and spiritual levels.

After performing one of the Basic Relaxation Exercises described earlier, visualize a field of color. You may also visualize the color as a flower, a light, a cloth, or a flame, such as a red rose, a blue sky, or a bright yellow sun. Visualize the color penetrating your entire being. In your mind's eye, feel the power that the particular color brings to your life, and how it can enhance your present-day reality.

Red arouses passion and desire. It is a color that is helpful to visualize when our energy level is low, or when we are lacking in courage or motivation. Red can help us to feel our connection to nature. Red also helps stimulate masculine energy and enables us to connect with qualities like strength, activity, assertiveness, protection, stability, realism and objectivity.

Orange mobilizes our courage to try something new. It enhances our desire for forward movement and to overcome obstacles. Orange also helps us to become more open to our feelings and energizes psychic vision.

Yellow has long been linked with stimulating intellectual activity and increasing mental capacity, and for this reason is a good color to meditate on when we have research to do or have an important decision to make. The color yellow rekindles dormant creativity and helps us feel more open to joy and humor. Drawing upon yellow also facilitates communication and helps us to become aware of new ideas.

Green is the color of healing and renewal. It enhances the desire for self-development and personal expansion, and facilitates our getting in touch with our innate optimism and enthusiasm. Meditate on the color green when you feel that your health needs improvement, or when you want to find a new direction in life.

Blue is viewed as a "quiet" color that facilitates receptivity and relaxation. Blue helps us to experience surrender in our lives, and access inner peace. The color blue also allows us to better feel our connection to the celestial realms and stimulates our so-called "feminine" qualities, such as sensitivity and intuitive recognition.

Indigo arouses the life force within (known in India as *Kundalini*) and helps us to integrate our sexuality with spirituality. Long connected to helping people become committed to one's spiritual path (as well as to embracing spiritual values in general), the color indigo inspires us to realize our inner divinity. Meditate on indigo if you want to find your spiritual direction in life.

Violet awakens both inner devotion and enhances our perceptions of universality and universal consciousness. It inspires soulmate recognition and helps us to develop deeper psychic and spiritual connections with our loved ones. Violet is a healing color. It also helps us to learn the value of forgiveness, so it is a good color to meditate on if you are angry or annoyed with yourself or another.

White is not technically a color, but it is composed of all the seven colors of the rainbow. Meditating on white helps us to perceive the universality of people and things and enables us to view life from a perspective of wholeness. At the same time, white awakens innocence and purity.

Rainbow Meditations

You can also meditate on all of the colors of the rainbow together. When you perform a Rainbow Meditation, imagine yourself sitting underneath its shining bands of color. Focus on each color one by one, and ponder the meaning it has in your life.

Rainbow colors can also be seen to resonate with different energy centers of chakras of the body (see *Chakra Meditations*, previous entry). Visualize each color around the corresponding chakra and think about what it means in that area of your life.

> Red: root chakra
> Orange: sacral chakra
> Yellow: solar plexus chakra
> Green: heart chakra
> Blue: throat chakra
> Indigo: brow chakra
> Violet: crown chakra

After several minutes, visualize these different colors vibrating in harmony with each other throughout your body. Gradually see the colors blend until they merge to become a field of pure, white light. Feel the energy of this white light permeate your entire body ("As seven colored rays merge in white light" - *Upanishads*). Feel the power, perceptiveness and inner healing that these wonderful combined energies provide. Gradually conclude your meditation by taking several deep breaths and stretches.

Meditations for Deepening Love and Enhancing Sexual Expression

Psychologists and others who have probed the workings of the human mind have found that the power of the unconscious is much greater than we realize. Because the unconscious functions primarily from our emotional memories and deep psychological patterns of which we are often unaware, its workings are not readily available for us to clearly see.

When we want something to happen or consciously believe in a hope or idea, we often find that our experience is different or even opposite of our conscious desire. As a result, we often feel disappointed and victimized. This is because our unconscious fears and attitudes have a powerful impact on our outer reality, no matter what our conscious desires may be. For this reason, it is important for us to try to make the unconscious *conscious*. One of the best ways to achieve this is through meditation and creative visualization.

The following meditations are based on the book *Lovelight: Unveiling the Mysteries of Love and Romance*, by Julia Bondi and me (Pocket Books, 1989). It is most effective when practiced after several minutes of deep breathing and relaxation.

Letting Go

All of us are carrying around fears, anxieties and other emotional baggage from our past. These inevitably project themselves into our relationships. The following meditation is designed to help us free ourselves from these negative images and feelings. It can best be practiced in a quiet setting with candlelight.

> You are going to take a trip to a special resort which is located in an area well known for its hot springs and healing waters. Surrounding this mountain retreat is a soothing pine forest. You are going to remain at this retreat for as long as you wish for

healing and rejuvenation.

Imagine yourself at the resort. You are walking through the pine forest and see many separate streams which flow into one large and beautiful pool. The air is crisp and clean. It has the scent of freshness. You instinctively know you will be able to heal yourself completely in this sylvan setting.

As you pass the streams, you see a small sign identifying the symptom which the waters will purify. There is a stream for every possible fear, including yours. By bathing in these waters, you will be able to experience a complete release of all the negativity from both your present and your past. Remove your robe and ease yourself into the stream that suits your needs. Remain in the running water until you feel yourself totally cleansed.

When you feel ready, proceed to any other stream which will heal the fears that you experience. After you have been cleansed by the healing waters, you feel ready to immerse yourself in the pool of self-love. You dive into the fresh, clear water and find that it is just the perfect temperature for you. There are bubbles of effervescence teasing your skin.

You immediately begin to relax and feel refreshed. The pool of self-love is the ultimate healing. The waters have washed away all beliefs and attitudes that have caused stress and negativity in the past.

You can perform this meditation whenever you wish. Each time you do it you will feel a deeper level of

179

cleansing. Experiment with the streams to see which ones you require at any particular time. Always finish the exercise with a swim in the pool of self-love into which all the other streams flow.

Experiencing Sexuality

Getting in touch with our sexual feelings is natural, appropriate and expansive. It is vital for our health and well-being on physical, emotional, mental and spiritual levels.

I.

Visualize or feel a flame of red energy in the root chakra which burns brightly in the sexual organs, suffusing them with warmth. This is the sexual fire which now can be expanded in an upward spiral of fire towards the higher chakras. The flame should be moved upward one chakra at a time until there is a spiral of fire (which is often experienced as sensual heat) warming and suffusing the entire body.

II.

See or feel a serpent coiled at the base of the spine. Like the snake charmers of the East, vocalize either the chant "HUM" vibrating through the body or the "OM-TA-MA-RA-OM" which balances all the body's energies. As you make these sounds, see the serpent gradually rising up through the chakras one by one until the serpent's head has reached the crown chakra while the serpent's tail is located in the root chakra and its body coiled throughout the intermediate chakras. Feel the power and undulating movement of the serpent.

The image of the coiled snake rising in an unfolding spiral was used extensively in ancient cultures (especially in Egypt and India) as a symbol of the creative unfolding spiral of life energy. Because the snake sheds its skin and emerges from it reborn, snakes were seen as symbols of transformation.

III.

See or feel the universe as a pool or reservoir of unlimited primal sexual energy out of which all creation has come. Feel yourself linked to that reservoir with a silver cord (like an umbilical cord) entering the body at the root chakra. With the aid of a pump, you can utilize as much of that energy as you want and need at any time. There is a switch on the pump which you can turn on or off at will. Feel the energy pumped up through each chakra, filling it with warm, vibrant light and pulsating energy. This enlivens you.

IV. Attunement with our Partner

This simple technique enables us to share with our partner on an emotional level. It is most effective when used just after we have done one of the previous exercises on chakra stimulation. Both partners can sit facing each other, and perform the following affirmations in turn:

> *Root*: "I give you (or I share) my support and
> my strength."

181

Sacral: "I give you my sexual desire and my
   passion."
Solar Plexus: "I give you my needs and my
   power."
Heart: "I give you my vulnerability and my
   compassion."
Throat: "I give you my truth and dialogue."
Brow: "I give you my vision and wisdom."
Crown: "I give you my soul and inspiration."

V. Meditation for Male-Female Energy Exchange

The following meditation is slightly more involved, and is designed to help us feel our own sexual energy as well as that of our partner. It helps us become more conscious of our roles as channels for the universal masculine and feminine polarities of cosmic creation.

The partners sit comfortably and face each other with their eyes closed. They should breathe quietly and deeply from the diaphragm until both feel relaxed and centered.

After several minutes of relaxation, the man begins to imagine himself as the masculine power of the Sun: the Sun God in his chariot of fire with blazing golden energy surrounding him and radiating outward.

The woman can visualize herself as the feminine power of the Moon: the lunar Goddess in a crescent boat on a lake of emotion. Silver lunar rays glow and shimmer from her body, the lake and her boat.

Ideally, each partner is to feel and see their respective images of themselves at the same moment, taking the time needed both to see the image in their mind's eye and feel its energy throughout their bodies.

After this image becomes clear, each partner should then draw the essence of this solar or lunar light into each energy center (beginning at the root chakra) and proceeding to the sacral, solar plexus, heart, throat, brow and crown, until each chakra in the male radiates golden solar fire and each chakra in the female glows with a silver lunar shimmer. This phase of the meditation can take several minutes, and need not be rushed.

When these energies suffuse the chakras, the couple should join hands. Each partner can begin to give to the other from each chakra beginning with the root. This is best accompanied by verbalizing the statement "I bless you with my light" while both partners watch that light slowly move to the partner's chakra.

In the male, the center of each chakra is to remain golden, but with a silvery shimmer surrounding it, a gift from his partner. In the female, her silver energy will be surrounded by an aura of golden light given to her by her partner.

The man begins at the chakra located at the base of the spine, giving this energy to his lover, and she follows doing the same for him. Then she gives her lover the energy of the next chakra and then he shares his energy with her. This process of reciprocal exchange reverses at the next chakra and continues until the crown chakra is reached.

VI. Finding the Purpose of the Relationship

On an individual basis, each partner can take a journey into the world of imagery through creative meditation. After performing one of the Basic Relaxation exercises described earlier, you begin at the entrance to a large forest where there are a variety of trails. Each trail is marked with a sign marked "Soul Purpose," "Past-Life Connection," "Present Opportunity," "Solution to Existing Problems" or other signs of your choosing.

Each time this meditation is done, we can choose the path on which we most desire to tread. Once we have chosen the path, there are arrows or signs before every curve in the path. These signs not only point the way, but offer a clue, a hint, or other piece of information which helps us deal with our question.

At the end of the path is a clearing, where we discover a beautiful shrine, temple or church. Steps are leading up towards the entrance of this holy place, where a guide awaits with the knowledge and wisdom we need about the path we have chosen.

Take this journey of imagery alone at first. After several such journeys, invite your partner to join you. At first, this will be done as a visualization so that you feel comfortable with your partner participating in this journey. At a later time you can sit together and take the journey together in person. After a while, the answers you seek will begin to appear. They will reveal more as your relationship deepens and grows.

VII. Finding Your Soulmate

Most of use desire to find a partner with whom we can share our lives totally, yet we don't know how to go about finding him or her. The following meditation and imagery technique will prepare you for the experience of finding your soulmate.

After performing one of the Basic Relaxation exercises described earlier, imagine yourself going into a complex which houses a powerful computer. The computer contains all the information available in the world. Its database is universal, and contains a complete dossier on every person alive.

As you enter, a person arrives to greet you. You are treated as a special guest. As your host explains the incredible capacity of this computer, you are told that it is entirely at your disposal. You are then asked to be seated and are offer a special request form for the ideal mate. The staff is available during this process to provide whatever assistance you require.

On this form you visualize yourself listing all of the qualities that you desire in a mate, such as sensitivity, sexual attractiveness, intelligence or a sense of humor. Once your request form is completed, a staff member will submit this data to the computer for you. At this time, your host returns to assure you that nothing more need be done, since the computer will search all its data until it locates your ideal mate.

With complete confidence in the process, you return home to await notification. A short time later, a telegram arrives confirming that your request has been filled. Your soulmate is ready to meet you and will arrive with no further effort on your part.

By doing this meditation, you have achieved the expectation that there is an ideal mate for you. You also affirm that the universe is busy finding your mate and bringing that person to you. In addition, this meditation reveals that you have a right to request the relationship you want and expect the delivery of that relationship at the appropriate time in your life.

A Group Meditation

The following meditation is practiced every morning at the National headquarters of the Theosophical Society in America, in Wheaton, Illinois. According to Dr. John Algeo, the former National President, this meditation helps the workers at the headquarters to focus better, increase their awareness of each other individually and the group, and to link themselves with other Theosophists throughout the world.

Although the following meditation is designed for a specific group, it can easily be adapted to be used by others.

The meditation is conducted according to the following pattern:

1. Each person becomes "centered," thinking of the center within themselves that is quiet and balanced, where the confusion and noise of daily life does not enter. At the same time, they are connected and whole, realizing their interconnection with all life.

2. All members of the group strive to feel harmony with one another and with the life around them: people, animals, trees, rocks, and more subtle forces of nature (devas) as well.

3. They attune themselves with all of the other members of the Theosophical Society, both as individuals and as groups, both in the United States and around the world. Members of the Theosophical Society are all linked through their international

186

center in India, and are also connected through their dedication to the First Object of the Society, which is:

To form a nucleus of the universal
brotherhood of humanity without distinction
of race, creed, sex, caste or color.

4. They think of the great teachers of humanity whom they call the Masters of the Wisdom, who inspired the foundation of the Society.

5. They think of the Light of wisdom and compassion, of creative power and peace, which shines through those great teachers, so that it may enlighten all beings everywhere.

6. They hold in mind persons who are troubled in body or mind and sent to them and to all in need thoughts of healing and wholeness. At this point, the names of people in need are read aloud by the person conducting the meditation.

7. The meditation ends with members of the group reciting aloud the universal invocation written by Dr. Annie Besant, the Society's 2nd International President:

O hidden Life, vibrant in every atom,
O hidden Light, shining in every creature,
O hidden love, embracing all in oneness,
May each who feel themselves as one with thee
Know they are therefore one with every other.

Acknowledgements

The author would like to thank the following individuals for their help in the successful completion of this book. To Yi-Shan Shei for her illustrations and for being the model for the meditations photographs; also to Rachel Benshmuel, Thomas Laubscher, Stuart Rynsburger, Bryan McAllister and Victoria Moran for their ideas and inspiration.

If any required acknowledgements have been omitted, or any rights overlooked, it is unintentional and forgiveness is requested. If notified, the compiler will be happy to rectify any omissions.

About the Author / Compiler

Nathaniel Altman is a Brooklyn-based writer, teacher and counselor who has authored more than twenty books on peace studies, healthy diets, alternative healing, nature, spirituality and relationship.

His books include *Eating for Life* (Quest Books, 1973, 1977; Vegetus 1984), *Ahimsa: Dynamic Compassion* (Quest, 1980), *Sacred Trees* (Sierra Club Books, 1994, Sterling Publishing, 1999, Gaupo Publishing 2017), *The Twelve Stages of Healing* [with Donald M. Epstein, D.C.] (New World Library, 1994), *The Deva Handbook* (Destiny Books, 1995), *The Little Giant Encyclopedia of Meditations and Blessings* (Sterling Publishing, 2000), *Healing Springs* (Healing Arts, 2000) *Sacred Water* (HiddenSpring, 2002), The Nonviolent Revolution (Gaupo Publishing, 2017) and five books about the art and science of hand analysis, including *Palmistry: The Universal Guide* (Sterling Publishing, 2009; Gaupo Publishing, 2017).

A student of metaphysics for over 40 years, Nathaniel is a writer, lecturer and workshop leader. He served as a faculty member at the Krotona School of Theosophy in Ojai, California, and has appeared on over 150 radio and television programs throughout the USA, Australia, Latin America and Europe. His articles have appeared in a variety of publications, including *Good Housekeeping, Natural Health, Well Being, Free Spirit, Vegetarian Times* and *USA Today*.

Also in this series

The Spiritual Tool Chest

Volume 2
Prayers and Blessings

Gaupo Publishing
Brooklyn, New York
www.gaupo.net

192

www.ingramcontent.com/pod-product-compliance
Lightning Source LLC
Chambersburg PA
CBHW070955040426
42443CB00007B/516